YOUR FIRST GUN

Should you buy one and join
60 million safely armed
American homes?

Packed with good info
for every firearm owner

Alan Korwin

BLOOMFIELD PRESS
Scottsdale, Arizona

BLOOMFIELD PRESS

4848 E. Cactus #505-440
Scottsdale, AZ 85254
(602) 996-4020 Office
(602) 494-0679 Fax
1-800-707-4020 Order Hotline
info@gunlaws.com

GunLaws.com

ISBN-13: 978-1-889632-33-9

Photograph of the author by Jeremy Voas

ATTENTION
Wholesale discount pricing is available for anyone interested:
Just call, click or write to us for wholesale prices!
Put this book into the hands of people who need it.
Give the gift of life.

Every potential gun owner needs this book—
"It doesn't make sense to own a gun and not know the rules."

Printed and bound in the United States of America
at McNaughton and Gunn, Inc., Saline, Michigan

First Edition

TABLE OF CONTENTS

DISCLAIMER

This book deals with social and cultural issues involved in obtaining a firearm for private personal use and enjoyment. It is not a guide to legal possession, purchase, sale, transfer, ownership or use of firearms, issues with which all firearm owners and users should become familiar.

Guns are deadly serious business and require the highest level of responsibility from you. Firearm ownership, possession and use are rights that carry awesome responsibility. Unfortunately, what the law says and what the authorities and courts do aren't always an exact match, creating legal exposures you must be careful to avoid. You are strongly urged to find and consult with a qualified attorney and local authorities to determine the current status and applicability of the law to specific situations you may encounter. As you will rapidly learn if you look, qualified attorneys in this field are rare, and qualified local authorities are virtually non-existent. Local authorities of any type are extremely reluctant to discuss these subjects with you, on or even off the record. Such are the dilemmas of the gun owner in modern American society. *Caveat emptor.*

This book is not "the law," and is not a substitute for the law. The law includes all the legal obligations imposed on you, a massive volume of work. You are fully accountable under the exact wording and current official interpretations of all applicable laws, regulations, court precedents, executive orders and more, when you deal with firearms under any circumstances. This is a daunting challenge in today's world. Fortunately, most gun owners do not cross paths with the legal system, quietly and peacefully enjoy keeping and bearing arms, and unless and until they stumble into the world of law enforcement or the judiciary, they lead lives of blissfully quiet ignorance. Once that veil of silence is pierced however, they may find themselves in a world of hurt, bewildered and outraged at how convoluted, expensive and unjust the justice system has become. You should do everything you legally can do to avoid contact with that world.

The author and publisher expressly disclaim any liability whatsoever arising out of reliance on information or opinions contained in this book. *New laws and regulations may be enacted at any time by the authorities.* The author and publisher make no representation that this book includes all requirements and prohibitions that may exist, and *any opinions expressed are included for informational and educational purposes only.* Local ordinances, rules, regulations and policies that may exist are not covered and are the sole responsibility of you. **This book makes no attempt to discuss or describe legal obligations or requirements of any nature, which are your sole responsibility.**

This book is dedicated

to all who would exercise

The Litmus Test of Freedom

by choosing to safely and responsibly

Keep and Bear Arms

Safety Rules

Gun ownership, the shooting sports and marksmanship are among the safest pursuits in America. We keep it that way by learning and adhering to the safety rules. Before you acquire Your First Gun, take a gun safety class with a qualified instructor, so you too will be a safe and competent American gun owner.

1

Treat every gun as if it is loaded
until you have personally proven otherwise.

2

Keep your finger off the trigger
until your sights are on the target
and you are ready to fire.

3

Never point the muzzle at anything
you are not willing to destroy.

4

Know your target and what's beyond it
before squeezing the trigger.

5

Always think first and shoot second.

6

Different experts prefer different safety rules, no one set of rules covers all circumstances, and you and you alone are responsible for the safe operation of your firearm under all situations. There are no excuses. Once a bullet leaves the muzzle of your gun you cannot call it back, and you are responsible for its entire trajectory.

MY FIRST GUN

"I wouldn't get a gun until the kids were out of the house. Teen angst, friends visiting, suicide, lack of responsibility, showing off, ratcheting an argument, I couldn't justify the risks. I work at home alone. We get solicitors. Someone came by once and I turned him away, but I realized he could have forced his way in and I'd be helpless. That moved me toward getting a gun, but first, 'hardening' the house made sense to me, with a security door and an alarm. Also, the gun does me no good if it's locked up unloaded and safe. I keep it loaded in my home office, because that's where I spend most of my time. My husband went through a period of gun buying, and now he's got a collection, more than I even know about. I feel comfortable we've made the right decisions." –Mary A.

•

"It was Christmas 1967, I was 12 years old living with my parents and I woke up first and quietly walked into the living room to see what my sister and I got from Santa. There it was, sitting on its own gun rack, my brand new Revelation 20-gauge single-shot shotgun. I could hardly contain my excitement. I gently picked up the gun, broke open the action and checked the chamber, then closed it and put it to my shoulder. It was big and heavy but beautiful and swung with ease as I followed an imaginary dove in flight. I could hardly wait to fire it but I knew Dad would need to be with me. I awakened my sister and we both woke our parents.

"After breakfast (why did that take so long?!) Dad took me into the back yard and went over the safety rules again to make sure I knew them, handed me my first shell and told me load the gun. I carefully aimed at the soda can on the fence post and *boom!* shredded it with #6 shot. I can still remember that feeling, and the smile I got then I get now. Dad and I hunted dove and quail, rabbits and squirrels. My single-shot and his pump gun worked together to feed us and build a father-son bond that lasted a lifetime. I still have that gun, and from time to time use it to target practice and rekindle old memories of a loving father and good times in the fields hunting together." –John Hard

•

"My first gun was a Marlin bolt-action single-shot .22. At 14, I was the oldest of my brothers and the first to get a rifle. It was a sort of rite of passage growing up in Texas. We had been shooting before, but this was the first time that I actually owned one I could call my own. It wasn't so much the gun that mattered, though that was certainly a thrill. It was our parents saying through this gift, 'You have earned this. You have reached an age where we can trust you and have confidence that you will apply what you have learned about guns and gun safety.' Though I wasn't a man yet, I was no longer a boy. This is the gift that represented that coming of age.

"Countless hours were spent in the pasture, shooting cans and cartons. When I let my brothers shoot it, I watched over them as my father watched over me. It was thrilling to know that my mother and father thought I was worthy of this gun. I've owned many guns and rifles since then, and the Marlin long since passed to younger nephews and nieces in our family. But as long as I live, I will never forget the thrill of holding my own rifle, and more importantly, what it meant to a young teenage boy so many years ago." –Jeff Young

CHAPTER ZERO

Not very long ago, a person's first gun came from family. Dad or an uncle, maybe a grandparent or an older sibling walked you through the exciting experience of getting your first real firearm, a sign of maturing towards adulthood.

Today, guns have become vilified and driven from the so-called mainstream by politicians who don't want you to keep and bear arms, and by the government school system and the "news" media, who exhibit fear of guns and precious little understanding of their usefulness ("social utility") or valuable place in history. You and your neighbors may have never come into direct personal contact with a real firearm in your lifetime, even though about 100 million of your fellow countrymen own and keep these valuable tools in more than half of all American homes.

Your decision to perhaps get Your First Gun is a good one, and when you go about it properly, it is a rewarding and fulfilling decision, putting you in league with those 60 million American families that keep and enjoy firearms.

In times when a person or family kept household firearms as a matter of routine, a first gun was typically a small rifle or shotgun for a young boy, a right of passage and an eagerly awaited day when Dad would take junior out back to try out the coolest new implement a youngster could have. For many, it arrived under the Christmas tree.

Perhaps soon, Independence Day will turn into a gift-giving holiday for such a treasure... firearms are certainly a grand tradition of the 4th of July! Celebrate freedom with fireworks and firearms! The 4th of July begins National Training Week, when Americans everywhere are encouraged to go to the range and practice marksmanship and gun safety.

In today's urbanized settings, chances are you'll be looking at a handgun of some sort for Your First Gun. They are also referred to as pistols, revolvers, six shooters, semi-autos, and sometimes by their brand names like Glocks or Colts, or by a bewildering array of nicknames. I'm going to focus on these handheld firearms to keep things simple at first, and we can look at long guns—rifles and shotguns, later.

It's important to first consider the idea of breaking the ice about simply buying and owning one of these somewhat mysterious things that fire ammunition, and the social and practical questions first-time owners ponder and need to answer. You certainly aren't getting any straight information from the popular culture.

> *Practically everything you see or hear about guns in the "news" media or in movies is just flat-out wrong.*

Once you own your first one and have had a chance to fire it you'll understand the truth of that statement better than you can possibly know it beforehand.

The media delights in using slang phrases like packing heat, strapped, and toting iron when talking about bearing arms, but these are derogatory slurs and show an anti-rights prejudice the media flaunts. People who know better never speak in such defamatory, gang-like terms when exercising a right as precious and traditional as the Second Amendment.

Guns are like shoes

People can give you all the advice in the world, but you still have to be the one to decide and pick out your own shoes for yourself. The same goes for a gun. It has to fit you. Don't make the mistake of just taking someone else's word for it and plopping down your hard-earned cash. At the very least, try it on for size before you buy.

How many different purposes do shoes serve? You've got house shoes, dress shoes, sneakers, beach shoes, sandals... they're all pretty different, and with good reason. And think about it—men, women and kids, young and old, need different ones. You can do a lot in flip flops, but you can't run very well in them. If you get invited somewhere nice you'll need polished leather or high heels. Guns are the same way. And yet, one pretty decent pair in basic leather can carry you through almost anything. The same goes for guns.

Because guns are pretty expensive, you may start with only one (most people do), but before long, you may realize it won't serve all your needs. If you're married, chances are you and your spouse will not prefer each other's choice. Because all guns are potentially lethal, any gun can save your life in an emergency, but some are better suited to that purpose than others.

Some guns are very expensive for practice or hard (or impossible!) for youngsters, oldsters or small-framed people to operate. Guns all have springs in them, and I've watched people struggle in vain to operate a gun whose springs were too tight for them to move. If you can't easily work Your First Gun you won't want to use it enough to really enjoy it, and you'll miss out on the best part of all this—*the fun of shooting*. Yup, shooting is a lot of fun. I'm guessing you didn't hear *that* too often in the "news" (though movies do get that right occasionally).

Like many first-time gun buyers you may be focused on self-defense and home safety. Think also about some of the other common and important uses of firearms like target practice and recreation—these are critically important uses especially for first-timers, to become familiar with the new tool you are getting ready to acquire.

**What's the best gun?
The one you have.**

**When you really need a gun,
any gun will do.**

Carrying a sidearm outside the home puts special demands on your choice that we'll look at later, which are significantly different from what might be your optimal choice for a home-defense gun. Competition and sport, hunting for food, durability and investment value are issues you'll think about too. If the natural draw of the shooting sports becomes appealing to you, you'll develop a collection, like golf clubs or running shoes.

Your First Gun though will have special meaning for you, like it does for everyone, so choose wisely. For now, we'll explore the options for the best all-around first purchase of a single general-duty sidearm that can serve as Your First Gun.

What caliber person are you?

Caliber is the thickness of a bullet. You can think of it also as the size of the hole in the front of a gun.*

A size-nine boot can be big or small, plain or fancy, but it's still a size nine for a size-nine foot. A .22-caliber gun, the same way, can be large or small, heavy or light, but it's still a .22-caliber gun. And just like a size-nine boot can come in various widths, with various heel types, a .22-caliber gun and its ammunition has varieties too. And just to make things confusing, the ammo for a .22-caliber handgun is called .22-caliber long-rifle ammunition. It makes absolutely no sense.

Here's the good news. You don't have to worry too much about caliber. But—

Gun stores, hard-core gun guys, even your relatives and friends who mean well, will turn you off right away with caliber talk. They can go on and on and never realize they lost you when they first started flinging around the insane numbering schemes. And the numbers *are* absolutely insane.

Because calibers have numbers and are about mechanical things, it can get as technical as rocket science, and it does. But you don't have to go there and most gun owners don't. So don't worry, be happy.

Look—you're going to end up basically with one gun, in one size, so you can pretty much forget about all the other confusing caliber stuff. You'll learn about *your* caliber, and that's plenty for getting started. You can get more detailed later if you want to.

And yes, caliber stuff is way confusing. It's not you, it's the subject. The numbers don't make sense, they just don't, so don't think it's you. They are not in any rational order, and there are lots of them. When .357 is bigger (much bigger!) than .380, that's irrational, I ain't lyin'. On top of caliber there is *ballistics*, the study of how different bullets fly through air, and that actually *is* rocket science.

And then there's the voodoo magic "stopping power" part. Some people get sucked into all of this hard, like birders, coin collectors or quilters, and dedicate their lives to it, join the clubs, go to the fancy conventions, there is no end to it. It's an option.

If you stay with the sport, or learn more than just enough to buy Your First Gun, or get serious about personal safety and self defense, you'll learn plenty about calibers, and you'll own more than whatever your first one is. But for Your First Gun, here's what usually happens.

Through a combination of rumor, hearsay, sincere advice, research, ignorance, guesswork, trial and error, this book and blind luck, you'll decide that a certain caliber is the right one for you. There is no "right" caliber of course, just like there is no "right" pair of shoes, just the one you decide to get. You do have to make a choice to own one, so you will. It will be just fine.

In early 21st century America, for sidearms, the common caliber sizes (which are the bullet's thickness in hundredths of an inch) are .22, .357, .38, .380, .40, .45, and the latest rage, 9mm (in millimeters, just to add to the illogic of it). If your first firearm is the handheld variety, it should be in one of these sizes.

Gun guys will tell me I left out some, and they're right, but you don't want to buy an oddball for Your First Gun, or pay a premium for oddball ammo you can't get easily. The caliber list is longer for rifles, and the numbers are even more weird, so I'm going to let you get that information elsewhere if you decide you need, say, a scoped bolt-action rifle, or maybe just a carbine for Your First Gun.

If you're convinced a shotgun should be your first, they don't call it caliber, they call it gauge, and I'll also leave that, and load size, to some other forum for you as well. You want an AK-47 commie gun with a banana clip because they're in the news and you're expecting the end of the world as we know it? They come in 7.62 x 39 and you're on your own.

You want my advice? The perfect gun for a newcomer is a .22. It is the easiest and least expensive on which to learn. It is the least frightening to shoot, with the least recoil, noise, blast, smoke and debris. It is easier to control and to gain proficiency with than any other firearm. It's every bit as real as any other gun, potentially just as lethal, and requires the same level of care as anything else you might buy.

The exhilarating experience of touching off your first round ever, that extra virgin feels-like-the-first-time first shot, should be with a .22, even if you end up buying some other gun. Idiots who hand a newcomer some high-caliber cannon, thinking it will be cool for a greenhorn to experience the shock and awe of a mega load the first time out, have done more to turn off new prospects to the ranks of gun owners than hypocrite anti-rights zealots marching around with their joyful death-to-gun-owners signs. Start with a .22 to cross the threshold, and work your way up from there.

Technically speaking: By thickness I mean diameter. I'm doing my best to limit complexities in this book. You want complex? Look up the *ogive* of a bullet.

As for *the hole in the front of the gun*, that phrase made the gun guys go crazy it's so inaccurate. The opening is called the *muzzle*, and it is a complex shape indirectly related to caliber.

The opening in the long part, the *barrel*, through which the bullet passes, called the *bore*, actually has high parts called *lands* and low parts called *grooves*. The caliber is usually measured from land to land, I told you this gets complicated, and you can do more research if you like.

Caliber plays a role in a gun's accuracy and power, along with many other factors, but at the distances you'll be practicing as a newcomer, and at the distances involved in self defense, it's not a great concern. Remember, all guns are potentially lethal, and that goes for all calibers. Many experts will tell you that *shot placement* is more important than endless talk about caliber, power, bullet weight, foot-pounds of energy, muzzle velocity, trajectory and other tech talk.

What does *less than lethal* mean?

A firearm stands at the end of the *continuum of force*, a long list of choices you have if you are attacked and choose to defend yourself. A gun is a choice of last resort, for use only when innocent life or limb is instantly at risk. Situations often present options that are lower on the force continuum. It is morally wise and generally legally required to use the least force possible to safely control a situation you are in.

Less-than-lethal options include things like pepper spray, stun weapons, audible sirens or whistles, various striking objects like clubs and handheld devices and other defense tools from tactical flashlights to Oriental fighting weapons. While you're spending time thinking about guns it would not hurt to put a can of 20-foot wasp spray near your front door.

Less-than-lethal options also include awareness training, hand-to-hand techniques and home "hardening" practices like lights, alarms, locks, cameras, motion detectors. Things that make you and your home a less attractive target to a miscreant intent on doing evil are all good ideas.

11₁ THE DECISIONS

Are guns for everyone?

No, they're not, and this is something the "gun community" and gun-rights advocates have a hard time accepting. People who are "into" guns, after so many years of being hounded and pounded about their rights are used to getting their backs up and being defensive about guns and gun rights. They can be quick to be defensive, so it makes them look and act like everyone should have a gun, and if you don't want one, there must be something wrong with you. Well, there isn't. Guns aren't for everyone. My relatives are good examples of this. Maybe some of yours are too.

One cousin, who shall remain nameless, freely admits she does not have the mental stability, emotional composure or personal fortitude to keep a gun. She could not trust herself with one. The specter of suicide and the immediacy of a gun's presence pose too great a threat to her and those around her and so *she is compelled to not keep one*.

Her former bouts of depression though now in the distant past exacerbate this reality for her. She would never be able to use one in any case, and would simply be at the mercy of an aggressor, and if that meant perishing, then so be it. That might seem horrifying or unnatural to you or another person, but not to her or countless others, and it is an important lesson to take, and an important license and freedom to grant her. It is her choice. Someone else could protect her. She can't do it herself.

No amount of argument, reason or discussion would change this for her, or perhaps for you. It is her makeup. Accept it. Her ability to survive a confrontation is low. It is who she is. It is her way. She lives in a major West Coast city where the people are largely like that, and they self-reinforce.

In Wyoming, by contrast, maybe everyone has a gun, except for a few crackpots. In some other state, it is different, and that's part of the beauty of this nation, it's called federalism. You can vote with your feet, and live in any of 50 states whose culture and style suits you and your preferences under the Constitution. Gun ownership is a guaranteed option, not a requirement.

As a free person it's her choice, or choice not to, or inability to choose, and you (and I) cannot morally hold it against her. You can lead a horse to water, and all that. There is no judgment involved, and it is not pejorative, it simply is what is. It may seem regrettable, and perhaps it is, but not to her, and in the grand scheme, not at all.

The only thing regrettable is when a person like that takes that inability or fear and turns it outward, seeking to disarm another person, as a psychological response or projection of their own inner feelings. She is fully entitled to her own gunlessness, but not to yours or mine.

This cousin doesn't do this but many other people do. That is not only regrettable *it is egregious*. It is a denial of another person's fundamental civil rights as a reaction to her own inadequacies—insecurities she is certainly entitled to have herself, but not entitled to use as a bludgeon against others.

"Disarming an innocent person is an act of violence," my old friend Craig Lindsay used to say. Maybe I shouldn't be getting quite so philosophical quite so early in this book.

> *"Disarming an innocent person*
> *is an act of violence."*

Why do I even want this thing?

A lot of reasons float through your mind while you consider getting Your First Gun, or wonder why anyone would. Watching TV and reading the "news" makes you think about it, but: *Most of what you see and hear in the popular media about guns is complete fantasy, and has nothing to do with how things really work.* When you finally do get your own, you'll be able to look back and see the truth in that statement.

The real answer to this question for most people these days is personal safety. If you've ever thought about what it would be like to face a deadly threat, you'd like to know you can defend your life or your family if it ever actually came to that. You may have actually been near such a situation and it shocked you awake. Happens to a lot of people.

Then again, a lot of people who talk to me about it are more just curious. The subject is literally everywhere, and while you can still just up and get yourself a firearm, maybe you should, especially since that option may not be so readily available in the near future—so many political forces seem determined to outlaw this right to keep and bear arms Americans have exercised for the entire life of the country.

The fear that the freedom to buy a gun—which we so openly enjoy at this point in time—might be confiscated by our own government, is a powerful motivation felt by many. Could government actually confiscate this right we now have and enjoy? Some say that's ridiculous. Others aren't as sure. Can government secure to itself such awesome power, simply by voting it to itself? Is that "government of limited powers"? If they can do that, is there anything they cannot do?

And that points to an even more remote motivator, one that drives far fewer first-time gun buyers, one that seems so highly unlikely yet nags at the darkest recesses of the conscious mind, a nagging fear deep down inside: What if the lunatic fringe on the right is right? Or what if maybe the Founding Fathers had it right? Or what if the rumors about the international scene are right? Or what if reports about those dark-age islamists are right? Or what if fears about the UN and a so-called new-world order are right? What if a disarmed public can be enslaved?*

What if an armed public is a free public, and is why America is what it is? Did the British army's effort at Lexington and Concord really mean what history books say, and the Colonists were right to defend those arms from government as they did more than two centuries ago?

What if there really is a balance of power between the people and their government, and that guns are the counterweight on that scale? What if the right to arms is a linchpin here in the one place that is the linchpin of freedom on the planet?

If any of that is true, maybe you ought to get a gun too, while you still can? Is that simply delusional, or is there any grain of rationale to that? Do the horrific genocides of the 20th century, all preceded by "official" gun confiscations, play into those equations at all? Research indicates that 262 million human beings in the 20th century met death at the hands of their own governments—the largest murderers of all by far—in what's known as *democide* (look up the term for a terrifying look a man's inhumanity to man).

Losing all of our freedom as we know it and encouraging a totalitarian regime bristling with nukes and armor-clad swat agents—is it a risk worth taking? When the only step needed to prevent it may be to buy a tool from any of thousands of retail shops selling the product—is that really any reason to buy Your First Gun?

> *Do keep in mind that this sort of wild-eyed supposition is quickly met with scorn and derision by reasonable mainstream people who are quick to point out that you simply can't shoot at F-16 fighter jets and tanks with pistols and hunting rifles. I'm the first to grant the point. I'm also quick to note that police remain reluctant to randomly sack individual homes or herd armed people into the streets, and that if massive military takeovers were ever to occur, all bets are off, but that's crazy talk. And fortunately, we're probably still a long way from F-16s attacking downtown Cincinnati, so let's just relegate those nightmare scenarios to Hollywood and our TV sets.

Yes, why do you even want a gun?

Let's leave sport, recreation, curiosity, the politics, human rights, the Second Amendment, balance of power, safety, genocide prevention, civil-upheaval protection, the national debate, the possibility that you won't be able to get a gun in the future, even the often overlooked or misunderstood point that guns are fun—let's leave all those reasons out for the moment. And cut to the chase.

What if your life depended on it. That's really the bottom line, isn't it? Everyone has fantasized about that. Everyone. Even rabid gun haters and that charming oxymoron—violent peaceniks. And it's not fantasy. Personal protection is real.

Peace and tranquility are maintained by force. Did you know that? Everywhere and for all time, in this best of all possible worlds, it is only by being able to exert force that you can have peace. As much as you may wish or believe otherwise, it's only because we are mighty that we have peaceful neighborhoods. It is an ugly truth, and I don't like it, but there it is.

That's because civilization unfortunately suffers from what I call the Four Horseman of Human Havoc: Angry, Hungry, Stupid and Wicked. They're out there. Always have been. They're even in you and in all of us. Most of us have most of it under control, most of the time. Some of us, and worse, some groups of us—like entire nations and coalitions—have it as their guiding principles. It is only by force that we maintain boundaries, and keep the Horsemen under control. Most of the time.

You know deep down inside, even if you have never thought about it consciously, that if your peace were ever broken by a late-night banging on the door, or anything really disturbing on the street, only force would protect you. Up until now you have hoped and prayed the force would not be needed. You've been lucky so far. Maybe police would get there in time. Or your spouse would save you. Or a strong stranger.

As you grow older and wiser, as the world seems to be a more dangerous place, as more of your peers and neighbors seem to be thinking it's a good idea, that's why you've decided to at least learn more about Your First Gun, and walk a path that more than 100 million Americans have walked. It turns out to be a very nice stroll.

Take Two: "No one is going to hurt my baby. If anyone tries they're going to have to get through me first. I'll scratch their eyes out." What kind of a mother would you be if you didn't stand up to guard and protect your child against all the whack jobs and crazies out there.

Preparing to scratch out eyes is commendable, sorta, pretty gory I suppose, but also pretty lame from a practical point of view, and not a very well thought out plan. If you're prepared to act like that—and society does encourage you to take direct action to protect your children—it would be wise to think a bit more about the plan. This is not easy thinking, but if you value your children as you should, it is important.

Keep in mind that until your child can walk, a gun kept safely in the house poses little problem for the child and presents a great increase in safety for the entire household. When the child becomes mobile, changes become necessary. A host of gear and strategies are available to continue the whole-house safety strategy. The book *Gun-Proof Your Children* is a must-have if you have young kids in the house, even if you have no gun—because your neighbors probably do, and you'll go visiting. That moves you to plans and thinking that go well beyond Your First Gun.

Take Three: You haven't needed a gun all these years and the chances that you'll need one now that you've decided you want one are about the same, pretty near zero. Sure, you might end up needing one, and you'll have one if the remote chance it becomes necessary, but man oh man, guns are fun! This is a fact gun owners know that is totally blacked out for the gunless by our hopelessly biased and uninformed media.

All the screws and bolts, moving parts and machinery that draws men to cars and anything mechanical are there. Every aspect of empowerment in the women's movement is there. If you can sit around and talk football for hours, wait till you see what gun talk is like. If you seek parity and equality wait until you find out what The Great Equalizer really means.

When you read *Babes With Bullets*, and learn how a woman in midlife discovered a new pursuit and world of friends, you'll wish you had entered this world sooner. There are even syndicated radio shows with just the right names—Gun Talk, and of course Armed American Radio—and now I'm going to get in trouble with all my friends with radio shows who I'm not listing. Drat. Google it.

I don't ever want to have to use a gun, so why even think about getting one?

No rational person ever *wants* to have to use a gun. You use a gun because you *have* to, God forbid, not because you want to. A person uses a gun because your life depends on it, that's the only reason. That's the only reason the law allows, that's the only reason morality allows, that's the only reason to ever consider *needing* a gun.

> *The choice to actually use a gun or not,*
> *to save a life in an emergency, remains yours*
> *right up to the ultimate moment*
> *that no one wants to face*
> *and everyone is tantalized by.*

You don't ever want to have a fire either, but you get a fire extinguisher, because it's prudent. You don't want a flat tire, but you carry a spare. A gun is just a life preserver, nothing more, nothing less, if your only focus is limited to the narrow "have to use" issue.

People who can overcome the fear mongering in the daily news and their own internal doubts, see the social utility of firearms, which we discuss later in this book, and rationally think about the indispensible aspects of firearm ownership, which have served this country well. Firearms do serve purposes besides the tragedies they flaunt in the news.

Now, virtually everyone who gets a gun never shoots anyone, so don't worry, this is almost never an issue. When people say the only purpose of a gun is to kill people, it suggests that all our guns are defective, because they've never killed anyone. That bumper-sticker put-down is wrong on its face—the only legitimate purpose of a gun is to protect people.

> *Virtually everyone who gets a gun*
> *never shoots anyone.*

That's not much comfort though for people who ask the ultimate question about gun use (and everyone does ponder it). It is a huge factor because it's so remote—your ownership (or lack) of a gun is unlikely to lead to the need to use it. Most people get through life without having to shoot their way out of a convenience store.

And you can of course own a gun, face death with your loaded gun in your hand, and choose to die rather than shoot at an attacker. Or let your child be murdered while you stand idly by, armed, with a clear shot on the attacker. That choice remains yours right up to the ultimate moment that no one wants to face and everyone is tantalized by.

The old joke, again way to wry, is about the old man, who needed a permit just to have a gun, and he gave his up after many years because he kept paying the tax, called a "fee," 'cause he never got nothin'.

I never needed a gun before, why get one now?

Maybe you shouldn't, and maybe you don't need one now. And maybe you never will. I hope you never will, and you should hope you never will too. It's like a fire extinguisher. You don't get one because you need it. You get one hoping you'll never need it. It's the not having one that's kind of dumb. It's insurance against what you hope will never happen. Pray you will never need it.

"We grow too soon old and too late smart." That's what my Czechoslovakian superintendent and babysitter used to say to me when I grew up in the Bronx. That's why.

*It's always better to avoid a gunfight
than to win one.*

With the increasing threats in the world, the growing numbers of loons running around loose and the decay of morality, with the breakdowns of society at its fringes, and the lawlessness that happens more easily after storms and civil disturbances—those are among the reasons people are thinking about finally getting themselves a firearm. In America, people used to have firearms as a matter of course. We went through a period of urbanization where this was no longer the case. That trend is now reversing and people are rediscovering the wisdom of having a personal firearm, just in case. That's why you're reading this book. Choose wisely.

Where would I even put the thing?

Every new gun owner runs this question over and over and considers the possibilities. There are no perfect answers, because you have to balance a variety of competing factors. You need to keep the gun protected from unauthorized users, away from curious visitors and yet readily accessible in case of emergency. No two homes are alike and you must consider where you spend most of your time at home, or where you consider your greatest vulnerabilities to be.

For many people that's in the bedroom at night, or in a home office, a kitchen area or a centrally located living area. This points out why people often feel the need to have more than one firearm in a home. People frequently do not like to discuss where they store a firearm, because it gives up *tactical advantage*. If your firearm ever turns up missing, the people you told, even your best friends, like it or not, automatically become suspects.

You will arrive at a place you feel most comfortable with for yourself and other adult residents you live with and with whom you entrust this information. The spot will be out of plain sight, and if you change it a number of times before you are satisfied that is pretty normal.

If you decide you want your gun (or guns) under lock and key affixed to the floor or walls, give the decision a lot of thought ahead of time, so you don't end up repairing your home more than once, and know any local laws on locking up your firearms. The ultimate safe storage calls for gun safes and gun locks. This is balanced with common-sense wisdom from Col. Jeff Cooper, who noted that, "A gun that's safe isn't worth anything." Be sure to comply with the law.

The whole idea of having a gun seems positively overpowering, is that just me?

The instant lethality of a gun is something you must come to grips with if you are going to get one. People deal with this all the time. If you don't think you can, then of course, guns are not for you. It's a decision each person must make on their own.

A mature well-adjusted adult typically handles this with the same composure as being in control of motor vehicles, power tools, kitchen knives, or even being in high places near steep drops where a false move is as instantly lethal as a loaded firearm. It's a scary thought but one we manage to come through with no problem. Guns however pose a particularly powerful conundrum.

The idea that you are free enough to actually buy a gun, that no power on Earth can stop you from doing this, this is indeed an awesome thought when you think about it. This puts all the vague arguments and TV rants into crystal-clear focus. You can hold this awesome power right in your own hand for a stack of cash and a simple decision. That is the power of this freedom.

Americans have and embrace this freedom to keep and bear arms that people in other parts of the world do not, and the world knows it.

> *Don't think for a moment that gunless people*
> *on the entire continent of Africa or Arabia or*
> *across communist China or anywhere else*
> *are safer because their right to arms*
> *is aggressively suppressed*
> *by governments there.*

You have something of enormous value in this guaranteed civil right, of which most of the world can only dream. Yes, it is tremendously powerful, this "palladium of liberty."

That thought helps put things into perspective. This freedom and your right to arms here is awesome in every sense of that word, and does contribute to our personal safety and the safety of our neighborhoods. *Many people are uncomfortable with that level of gun freedom and would restrict it for you, because they are uncomfortable with it for themselves.* It is no wonder you feel this great weight as you contemplate Your First Gun. Consider this mental exercise.

Why not just ban guns for those who would ban guns for us? How well would that sit? Let those who would ban guns sign up to be permanently banned from firearms possession for themselves—for their entire lives. How would that test freedom's mettle? It's a free country, they should be able to choose that for themselves if they wish. "I hereby choose to be forever banned from firearm possession of my own free will, under penalty of felony arrest and conviction. Sign here." I just don't think they can morally choose that for you or me or for anyone else. A thought experiment like that puts the fire behind this right we hold so dear, and the power you feel welling up as you move closer to wielding it yourself.

How do I explain this to my spouse?

The decision to get a gun starts in your own mind alone— married, single, young, old, male, female, it doesn't matter. It starts with you and grows for a while before you mention it to anyone. If you're married, the subject has to come up in that context. How you broach the subject is up to you.

And it's not about explaining, it's about agreeing. I don't prefer seeing a one-sided decision on bringing a gun into a household but it does happen, whether it's the man or the woman wearing the pants.

Well actually, I've thought about getting a gun, but my spouse says "No."

If your house is strictly divided on the issue, I'd have to say wait, probably. Internal friction and discord, or a lack of agreement may not be a good environment into which to bring a gun. Don't feel too bad, it's not uncommon. Women are often (though not always) more poorly educated on this subject than men, despite the empowerment the women's movement preaches, at least on the surface, unfortunately. It's popular to say guns are a man's thing, but that's untrue. It's about education. Feminism is insular, and empowerment is selective, as studies and simple observation shows. Despite this, women are often ahead of male partners on the gun issue. Often, it is the woman who presses for a gun at home.

Whichever partner harbors the doubts, the best advice I can offer is to let that person read this book, or others aimed at piercing the veil of ignorance or fear. If it's a woman, try *The Cornered Cat*, or *Armed and Female.* Suzanna Gratia Hupp's experience in the Luby's massacre is revealing, *From Luby's to the Legislature*, or *Babes With Bullets*, by a woman who saw the light in midlife, and became a firearms enthusiast, trainer and competitor. Some of the books with life-or-death tales of people who survived because they had a firearm might help. They're all listed in the back of this book.

That question about spouses has a whole lot of hidden dynamite in it. Personally I'm for as open a relationship as you can get, and if you can't discuss getting Your First Gun with your spouse, that might be a really good reason to put off getting one. How can you have one if you can't even *talk* about having one? In my house, I can't even do that with a toaster oven. Harmony first, cookware second.

On the other hand, because being gunless can be so very dangerous, some people I know have chosen to get one anyway, against the wishes of a spouse. They keep it safely and secretly secured without the spouse's knowledge, and in an emergency, it's there. Ideally, your spouse should be on board before you proceed, and really, you both ought to make the choice together, and know how to shoot the thing.

Isn't it dangerous to keep a gun in the house?

Yes, of course it is. That's the whole point. Your biggest question may be deciding if you can manage that risk as so many millions of others routinely do, for the same reasons they routinely do. If you feel you lack the physical skill, or cannot manage your impulses, strife, your own rage or feelings of inadequacy, the conflicts you normally encounter from day to day, then maybe gun ownership is not for you. Some folks do not have the mental attitude, the character, the peace of mind, composure, the maturity, the whatever it is it takes to safely keep and bear arms as a free and independent adult American citizen. If so, don't do it.

There is also often, though not always, a political dividing line here, separating the left and right to some greater or lesser degree. The composure to keep and bear arms seems to come more naturally to conservatives and less so to liberals, if casual observation is any gauge, no? At any rate, if guns and gun ownership make you feel squeamish and uncomfortable then this book is not for you, and neither is gun ownership. Stop reading right now. Put these thoughts out of your mind. Do not let a firearm into your home.

But it's also dangerous *not* to have a gun in your house, as I've pointed out. Somehow, about 60 million American homemakers have managed to do it safely. They have it there in the event of a dire emergency. While people with guns have caused tragedy—a fact you know from incessant pounding from your TV set—people with guns also save lives every day—a point your TV suppresses. The true purpose of guns is to protect people, and they are extremely good at doing that. *When you really need a gun, little else will do.* That's why so many people keep one. At least one.

That's why it's good that gun ownership is *optional*. You are not *required* to keep and bear arms, as some vigorous gun-rights people would like to mandate. Gun ownership is not a requirement of citizenship, as it is in some nations. It is a choice free citizens can make, on their own.

What about all the magazine articles I've seen—aren't they pretty convincing that gun ownership is a bad thing?

According to Phil Intheblank, Ph.D., M.D., Professor Emeritus of Bullet Holistic Studies funding at Harvard University, a recent study shows that civilians' guns lead to more deaths and tragedies, and no amount of training can reverse this dire trend... does that sound familiar? It's one of the oldest tricks in the magazine journalism play book. We all use it. The editors expect it. You quote some official-sounding expert somewhere, whose single quote sounds like it supports your story. Add to it a recent study—of course it's a recent study— that supports the quote. And your persuasive story runs in a top-selling magazine. Well that's why they call them *stories*.

You can find so-called experts who will support any story, or any thesis, with a recent study that supports anything. That's not science. It's "yellow" journalism. Convenient, magazine-selling tripe designed to convince and be titillating and promote an agenda. You should ignore it. It means little.

These people quote the same old tired "experts," heavily credentialed but actually died-in-the-wool advocates like Garen Wintemute, David Hemenway, the CDC, VPC, MMM, BCPGV, I know the names, you perhaps don't, they appear regularly, they're in the Rolodexes, the reporters don't always clearly describe their affiliations because that would rip credibility from the story. Real research doesn't look anything like magazine articles. Slightly more credible is, "A recent study of 15 studies on the subject suggests that..."

And real research is piled high on both sides of this issue. Like I said in the statistics segment of this book, your rights aren't subject to statistics. The world could decide that Christianity has done more harm than good—as if that could be determined or subject to measurement—and it would not change your ability or right or the righteousness of your desire to pursue Christianity, or any religion of your choice. That is your unalienable right. Do not for a moment think that your rights are subject to cost-benefit analysis.

The same is true for your right to your life and your right to defend your life. That's why the Founders, in their wisdom, recognized the right to keep and bear arms in the U.S. Constitution. If you study the Second Amendment, delve into the meaning of the Militia and all the details surrounding it, you will come to understand that your right to your own life, and your right to its defense, on a personal, community and national scale, are at the heart of the right to arms, not just firearms, but all arms that an individual can possess. Gunlaws.com has an entire library's worth of reading on this subject in its political and rights pages.

All the statistics have me confused—does a gun really make me safer?

If you've noticed that the statistics are confusing you're right, they're hopelessly confusing. I believe that's deliberate, and it begs the real question.

Your right to own a gun and protect yourself with it is not and should not be subject to a cost-benefit analysis. Even if there was a way to sort out the numbers and find the "true facts," your right to have a gun and use it to defend your life, your family, or simply possess it for all the legitimate purposes it serves is as fundamental as your right to possess a book, religious goods, any other private property, as many shoes as you like or anything else in a free society. People who tell you otherwise are fighting against the things that make this country the shining light of freedom that attracts the world to our shores.

> *Your right to own a gun and protect yourself*
> *is not and should not be subject*
> *to a cost-benefit analysis.*

The statistics from the Brady group and their allies very convincingly support their position that guns are basically bad, and no one should have any except the police, federal agents and government people who should have plenty. The numbers from the NRA and their allies also convincingly support the position that guns are good and everyone should be trained in the safe use of firearms whether you choose to own one or not. They can't both be right, right?

I don't believe any of this should be decided based on these conflicting sets of numbers. You, as a free man or woman get to decide for yourself. Read up on the numbers if you like, watch for all the discrepancies, and see if it helps you make this very personal choice. I doubt that it will. Either side can throw numbers at you all day long. In the end, your decision is made from a different perspective.

Your rights are better understood and stand more properly on moral, legal, logical, emotional, philosophical, historical, humanitarian, ethical, judicial and religious grounds, or based upon civil rights and your unalienable right-to-survive, than on fungible numbers manipulated to make points and support agendas. I've studied it hard. Read more here: http://www.gunlaws.com/faq.htm#howmany

There is no way I'm letting a gun into this house, so why even think about it?

That of course can be very dangerous.

It means your fear of a gun is greater than your fear of having a home that is basically defenseless. It means your fear of a gun is greater than your fear of a criminal with a gun. That may be irrational, and could be a sign that you suffer from *hoplophobia*, a morbid fear of weapons. The medical community is in denial about this serious malady, which afflicts tens of millions of people. Does it mean your fear of defending yourself is greater than your fear of being assaulted or killed? You need to think about that, and your family's safety.

In the event of a dire emergency, you can use a phone (if it's working) to call for someone else with a gun—an interesting paradox—if those people aren't busy, and are close enough to respond before the glass breaks, and have them risk their lives for you. The classic one-liner is: "When seconds count, the police are just minutes away." On a good day.

To paraphrase one of The Cartridge Family Band's songs, the police don't draw their guns, they draw chalk lines when you're gone. A lot of people actually prefer that option. They don't buy this book. How many times do you have to see police, all dressed up in battle gear, parading outside a crime scene too late to do anything, before realizing that the first responders are you, the victims at the scene, not the police who arrive afterwards to pick up the pieces.

The book *Dial 911 and Die* points out that police have no legal duty to protect you. This is true—by law—in all 50 states, despite what you may believe, or the signs on their squad cars that say *To Protect And Serve*. Every state's courts have reiterated the point, described state-by-state in that book. The school system fails to teach this.

The U.S. Supreme Court has repeated that legal point many times, most recently in *Castle Rock v. Gonzalez* in 2005. A woman's deranged husband, with a long history of abuse repeatedly threatened to kill his estranged wife's kids, and was now attempting to do so. She desperately pleaded with the cops to come and stop him, and the dispatcher went to lunch instead. The madman shot all three children to death.

When the case reached the Supremes, they said she had no case, in a 7 to 2 decision. The fact that a city sets up a police force does not obligate the city to protect everyone in it. Have a nice day. Cynical observers draw all sorts of self-defense conclusions about the value of police from this.

Now of course, having a gun in the house is dangerous too as I've already pointed out and you already know. It's supposed to be dangerous. It wouldn't be much good if it wasn't dangerous. The idea is to be enough of a responsible adult to be able to understand the dangers and manage them in a responsible way. One hundred million other Americans have figured out how to do that, so it can't be that difficult. You can too. Or you can decide not to. That's why you're reading.

If you feel or believe it is too difficult for you, then by all means, do not let a gun into your home. Learn more, think about it, and if you can't overcome the discomfort, or come to believe that you cannot manage or control your inner turmoil, then put this book down, go read a soothing romance novel, and forget about the whole thing. And find out you just cannot forget the whole thing. Ever.

At least, look into "less-than-lethal" options available to you. The book *The Truth About Self Protection* covers everything from planting cactus outside your windows to evasive driving techniques, and how to "harden" your home against home invasion. A gun is part of what's known as the *continuum of force*, and guns are at the very end of that sequence of events. Even if you're armed to the teeth, it's wise to know steps you can take before you resort to the ultimate arbiter of personal safety.

Wouldn't it be better just to ban guns totally so no one had a gun?

Yes, and I'm all for that. In fact, and this may seem odd, but *I'm basically for utopian pacifism*. I'm in favor of no weapons of any kind at all on the entire surface of the Earth, in an era of enduring peace, prosperity, harmony and abundance. I stand for total disarmament—but bad guys first. I did say this is utopian, right? A delightfully worthy goal, but impossible.

Until we can do that, I have to remain skeptical of any plan that says take away a gun from me—or from you if you want one—before we disarm the bad guys who already have them.

So the problem is, how do we do that? That comes down to The Four Horsemen of Human Havoc again: Angry, Hungry, Stupid and Wicked. Until we figure how to eliminate them, or at least bring them under total control, the good guys need guns. For their own safety and protection.

If you could eliminate all the guns in the world by waving a magic wand, the good guys would have to reinvent them to protect themselves from the bad guys using brute strength, clubs and swords. I wish we could eliminate guns just using laws, but we've already tried that and it doesn't work—guns are completely outlawed for outlaws, yet they're all totally armed. Arms outlawed, outlaws armed. Just like crack and smack. Go figure.

We could ban guns totally here in America, but that would do nothing to stop the communist Chinese and every other nation in the world from making guns (which they all do by the way) and smuggling them in here, in an iron river that would make drug traffic look like a small-town flea market.

The ugly truth is that the genie is out of the bottle. We can't go back to the days before guns, and wouldn't want to if you think about it—when Genghis Khan and Attila the Hun ruled by brute force. And it makes no sense to disarm or weaken innocent people like you and me before we can disarm all the miscreants, rapists, murderers and tyrants running loose.

The truth is, the world is a dangerous place. I don't like it, but there it is. Perhaps George Orwell put it best: "People sleep peacefully in their beds at night only because rough men stand ready to do violence on their behalf." Sometimes, in a pinch, you have to do the violence on your own behalf. I wish it weren't so.

What will my neighbors think of me if I get a gun?

Your neighbors are not part of this equation. Gun ownership is a private matter in this free country, as it should be. It's the same as with any other private or valuable property you own, like investments, or a second home, your jewelry, bank accounts, anything. You don't know if they own a gun, nor should you, unless they opt to tell you. Politicians who think they should publicize your gun ownership are crossing way over a line that should remain private. You can tell people if you want, but if you're nervous with a question like this, it's probably best to keep it to yourself, at least at first.

Maybe you're really asking, what will *you* think of you if you get a gun. You have been bombarded by so many conflicting messages on TV and in the so-called "news" as a gunless person that your emotions may be tied in a knot about gun ownership. While your fellow citizens have enjoyed firearm ownership for centuries without the moral or pragmatic dilemmas you may be wrestling with, for you, this is a momentous decision.

Your neighbors won't think any more or less of you because it's none of their business—and they won't know you've made the important and mature decision to take this step responsibly for yourself. To be able to protect yourself and your family in an emergency, that's a good thing, and a benefit to your community. And don't start thinking you're all-of-a-sudden a freelance cop either. Remember—the best gunfight is the one you avoid.

No one in my family has ever owned a gun before, so why me?

The times they are a changin'. Actually, the times have already changed, and what's happening is they are changing again. Have you seen the Oscar-winning musical *Oklahoma*, or a batch of old Westerns? Everyone in town used to own firearms, it was routine. If you're old enough to remember Walt Disney's *The Mouseketeers*, they used to prance around wearing a pair of six guns, twirling them in dance numbers, and Uncle Bob used to heft a shotgun over his shoulder. No one gave it a second thought.

Then we became so urbanized it fell out of vogue. Political correctness reared its head, and though arms kept us free, safe and defended our borders and interests, cookie-cutter suburban neighborhoods were a whole new ballgame. Now individualism and personal gun ownership are experiencing a revival. How's that for a century of change in a sentence or two. The tides of change blow.

The role of women in modern society are a major part of our changing trends. No longer stuck in a damned subservient role, "the great equalizer" has special appeal. Feminism and the growing freedom movement has empowered women and nothing is as empowering as firearm ownership. Competent ownership of a sidearm is liberating. Maybe you're just a product of your times, as are we all.

New York City mayor Ed Koch once said, "Nice guys who own guns aren't nice guys, even if they're nice guys." Wouldn't that apply to me?

When I lived in New York City, Ed Koch was the mayor and I thought he was a really nice guy. Now I know better. He was surrounded by guys with guns 24/7 so he didn't have to carry one himself. Of all the elitist, ivory-tower, sleazy, hypocritical removed-from-reality, statist power-broker, better-than-the-common-man pieces of bigoted trash a human being could utter, that remark takes the cake. And I'm being nice.

Mayor Koch relied on guns for his safety because he knew guns kept him safe. He knew he faced dangers but wasn't man enough to protect himself so he relied on others to do it for him. He could justify it because he was the mayor. Like so many people living in big east coast cities, where the harsh realities of life are removed like a steak under plastic wrap in a supermarket, he could make remarks like that. He had thousands of heavily armed police officers to keep the peace, and I'm in favor of that. But in the Black ghettos they maybe didn't think of it as Officer Friendly now did they.

The NYC police are now so overwhelmed they don't even show up for burglaries. They just take reports over the phone, so you can get the number you need to file an insurance claim. Nice guys own nice guns and show their nice friends how to shoot straight. Have a nice day.

I've got to keep it locked up 'cause I've got kids, so what good is it anyway?

This is a very important and delicate point.

I once heard Col. Jeff Cooper, often called The Father of the Modern Technique of Handgunning, say, "A gun that's safe isn't worth anything." And while he's right, a gun that's ready for it's designed purpose—to protect people—is a very dangerous thing. I repeat myself because it's important.

Massad Ayoob, considered one of the world's leading experts in the use of deadly force, has taught me and countless thousands of others that guns are dangerous, that they're supposed to be dangerous, and they wouldn't be much good if they weren't dangerous. So what do you do about this conflicting set of values?

There are two basic approaches—locks, and hiding. In addition, you can choose to be gunless while you have kids in the house, and people take this route. You can also choose to separate and hide the ammunition.

None of the solutions are perfect. If you choose to be gunless remember, with about half of all American homes armed, your neighbors on either side of you may have a gun, so if your child goes visiting, the potential danger re-remerges. Education in gun safety may be your best bet here. It is a national travesty that schools graduate students without any training in gun safety. A high-school diploma should require at least one credit in marksmanship. Also, Ayoob's book *Gun Proof Your Children* belongs in every parent's home.

You have no doubt thought about where you could effectively hide a gun in your own home, and it would be foolish for me to try to do that for you. Until your child can walk that's probably a reasonable option, and do consider nosy neighbors and visitors as well, who may just be looking for the sugar bowl or a TV remote. Some cool hideout gizmos are available too, like hinged picture frames, magnetic back-of-furniture grabs and hollow books.

Locks are now supplied with new guns sold from dealers or even given away at safety events and outdoor expos. These will prevent a person from using a gun, but they can be awkward to use in an emergency, you must have the little key to make the gun ready, and if a child or anyone finds the key the lock is overcome. Much better locks are sold, including touchpad lock boxes you can operate in the dark and bolt to a wall or floor. They all have their strengths and weaknesses. With a little investigation you'll decide what you feel is best for you. Like shoes, there is no perfect answer, no one size fits all, and no one can give the answer to you.

If your locale has gun-locking requirements you need to know them and follow the rules of course, and your local gun shop can fill you in on any details. The tightest interpretation of gun-safety procedures suggest always keeping guns under lock and key, even if this compromises your safety, which it does. Criminals will not comply with lock-up-your-safety rules of course, and so once again we find that rules made for the public, ostensibly designed to control problems, leave the problems uncontrolled.

What kind of gun should I buy?

This whole book beats around that big bush, so let me just make a few simple points here. For Your First Gun in this modern day and age, with almost all people living in a city or near one, which is 85% of us, I say your choice should be for a sidearm—a handgun. Some experts say it should be a shotgun or rifle (the other two main types of firearm). If you agree, go buy their books.

Sidearms come in two basic types, *revolvers*, and *pistols* (also called *semi-automatics* or *semi-autos*), and that's your basic choice, revolver or pistol. The media and anti-rights advocates like to talk about semi-automatics, because the uninformed think that means machine guns. It does not.

If you're a real novice and you're not good with mechanical things, a *revolver* may be best. It is the simplest type, the most reliable, has the fewest moving parts, and once it is loaded if you pull the trigger it goes bang. The downside is that it holds the fewest shots (usually six) and it is slower to refill (*reload* is the correct word). It is also easy to clean and doesn't have to be taken apart to clean (all guns need to be cleaned occasionally to work well, more on that later).

A *pistol* (or *semi-automatic* or *semi-auto*) is more popular these days and has a number of advantages. It holds more shots (between seven and 17 usually). It can be made smaller and it is flatter so it can be carried discreetly (concealed) more easily. The ammunition is held in a *magazine*, it slides out of the handle, and can be replaced quickly to reload.

The downsides come from the complexity of a semi-auto—it has a number of switches and moving parts that must all be in proper order to fire. You need decent arm and hand strength to pull back the gun's top, called the *slide*, to load the first piece of ammunition after you put the magazine firmly into the handle, before the gun will fire, and some people cannot do this.

Pushing the ammunition into the magazine also takes more hand strength than some people have, especially once the magazine is nearly full. Understanding how the gun might fire when the magazine is removed, or might not fire with the magazine inserted is downright confusing at first. And the safety switch on some pistols can't always be put on, but must be put off to fire. Different brands work differently.

A semi-auto pistol must be taken apart to clean properly, and then reassembled before it can be used. Gun dealers are used to people showing up with a sheepish look and a bag full of parts they can't get back together again. Pistols have a greater tendency to jam (stop working) than revolvers. Clearing a jam in either type of gun can be difficult and can put your life at risk.

If you can handle it, a pistol's advantages can outweigh its shortcomings. You can decide for yourself when you take a class, go to a range, check out a friend's personal firearms or go to a store or two and handle a few yourself.

How do I make sense of all the technical talk and numbers?

You really can't at first. You'll pick a caliber and gun type by your best guess and just break the ice. Everyone does. You jump in and get your feet wet. Only then, and after some practice, can you make a more informed decision. It's like shoes again. You get your first pair as an adult with high hopes they will perform for you. Likely, they do. Then you start to realize... bedroom slippers, back-woods trails...

If you have some gun-savvy friends you can make a few trips to the range with them and shoot their guns. Most gun-savvy people are delighted to take newcomers to the range, and show them everything they know (takes about ten minutes).

Then, you end up wanting to buy whatever it is they own, which is not such a bad way to decide. It isn't until later when you discover other arms that may be better suited to you for all sorts of reasons, and then you can sell, trade, or end up with the beginnings of a collection. It will answer a question that may have seemed impossible to understand earlier—why does a person need so many guns? And you may start to understand the bias in the "news" when they make breathless reports that a person had a collection of different guns. You may even get to that disquieting point yourself where you need a second gun safe because the first one is full. Don't laugh, it happens.

What if my spouse wants a different gun than me?

This mean you're coming along nicely. If you're in a situation where you and a spouse have both decided to make sure you can protect hearth and home, then you will very naturally arrive at the fact that one pair of shoes will not fit you both, and neither will guns. This is good. And it has plusses and minuses.

Your costs just went up. Whatever you figured a gun would cost you just doubled, as well as the initial grocery list of ammo and supplies you figured you'd lay in. You'll both need holsters. Whichever one of you likes to shop is about to get a joy ride.

One main reason to get two different smokewagons is hand size. And in another one of those politically incorrect inequalities polite society wants to ignore these days, women are usually smaller than men, so you will (at least statistically) end up with one bigger, heavier, higher-powered, more-expensive-to-own-and-fill-with-ammo gun, and a smaller, less-expensive-to-own-and-shoot, easier-to-handle-and-carry-discreetly, not-quite-as-loud smaller gun. This difference, for new gun owners, is an unparalleled learning experience.

What's the best kind of bullets?

Let's start by talking the talk. You mean what's the best kind of *ammunition*. Bullets are just the part of one piece (called a *round* or *cartridge*) of ammunition (*ammo* for short), that comes out of a gun. Ignorant people in the media talk about bullets because they don't know any better. They'll say, "he was found with a pocket full of bullets," which sounds silly to anyone who knows anything. You don't want to sound that way.

What's the best kind of ammunition?

Is Nike better than Reebok? Is Frigidaire better than Maytag? Each brand claims it is best in every business and ammo makers are no different. The major name brands are all fine and every one has its fans. Shopping by price is certainly one acceptable way to arrive at a choice.

For routine practice at the range inexpensive ammo is fine and saves money, but it usually leaves more burnt debris in your gun (all ammo leaves burnt residue in your gun), which is part of why it is cheaper, and will mean it needs more cleaning. As long as you stay with major brands reliability should not be a problem.

Cheap ammo is often imported from communist China, Russia, other former communist bloc countries, Mexico,

South America or other places where labor is cheap. Most of this is acceptable, but some can be corrosive to the parts inside your firearm, or unreliable. If you buy from a reliable store or brands you come to recognize you should be OK.

Reloaded ammo is made from brass casings that have been used (already fired by someone), cleaned and reassembled. If done properly it is fine and the price can be very attractive. Again, if you are dealing with a reputable source, reloads can save you a lot of money.

When loading your firearm to keep ready for personal defense, take a tip from police nationwide. They generally choose, and experts generally recommend factory-made premium-grade *hollowpoint* ammunition. This can cost double or even triple what average rounds cost, but since your life may depend on it, it is not a place for saving money or cutting corners.

This is designed to have maximum stopping power, to be least likely to pass through an attacker and hit anything behind that person, minimize the risk of ricochet and protect you best. If you want to see some fascinating but mind-numbing techno-speak, look up self-defense ammunition and prepare for a long read.

Although most folks consider premium self-defense ammo too expensive to practice with regularly, you should try some in your gun to make sure it works OK. Guns handle different types of ammo differently, and you want to know the ammo you load for personal safety works well in the gun you've chosen for self defense.

How much ammo do I need?

The wise aleck answer is more than you have. The hard answer in emergencies is you never have enough. The practical answer in terms of preparedness is you can always use more. My spouse's answer is, if you buy any more, you better not plan on storing any of it in the kitchen. The prepper's answer is that ammo has a shelf life of decades, is one of the best items for barter, and keeps going up in value. The "news" media's answer is that anything more than a single small box is a stockpile in an arms depot stored in an arsenal by a wing nut living in a compound who poses a danger to the civilized world. Sound familiar?

The commercial answer is that Americans buy between five and nine *billion* rounds of ammo every year, virtually all of which goes to peaceful purposes and into the number two participant sport in the country, ahead of golf (which is number three) by more than $1 billion a year. When you're at the range, it is easy to go through a few hundred rounds, though one box of 50 shells makes for a good casual hour of practice, and 1,000 rounds is not unusual for a high-intensity weekend of training at one of the better training schools around the nation.

Should I get a little gun?

I've heard this question in my travels, and here's the hidden question that's usually behind it, often from a shaky-voiced little old lady (no offense meant): If I just get a little gun, I could use it to scare off someone without having to really hurt them, right? And here's the answer: No.

First, any gun is potentially lethal. Secondly, bringing any gun into a situation, even if you think you're only acting in perfectly legal self defense, opens you up to a possible charge of aggravated assault or even attempted murder, so don't think a little gun means you've got less of a legal challenge before you. Third, since you can only bring out a gun if your life depends on it, the last thing you want to do is rely on some tiny underpowered unreliable embarrassing little mouse gun that you got because you were afraid to get any gun, and so opted for some cute pearl-handled virtual toy instead of a real firearm.

There is a legitimate place for a compact firearm for very discreet carry, like when you're wearing lightweight summer clothes, and gun makers have developed some rather tiny sidearms for this purpose. They are a little harder to shoot and control, but it's better to have one in a pinch than to be defenseless, and that's a different question than the one proposed for this passage.

How can I tell how much *stopping power* a gun has?

Stopping power seems like a really cool and powerful sounding phrase. Newcomers are fascinated by it, because it sounds like you should want as much of that magical stuff as you can get, right?

The research shows that in 98% of defensive gun uses (DGUs), the gun isn't even fired. There is a book by researchers Gary Kleck and Donald Kates, called *Armed*, that examines 13 of these major studies, showing between 700,000 and 2.5 million DGUs each year, depending on study size, time frames and other factors. The gun is mentioned, reached for, presented, or pointed, and its mere presence, or the fact that it is available, is enough to prevent an assault or stop a confrontation from occurring. I'd say that's a lot of stopping power.

But this question of stopping power from a newcomer's perspective implies how much brute force a gun and it's fired bullet has on a target, or more precisely on a person. In even simpler (but less accurate) terms, it's about how much *knockdown power* Your First Gun has. That's the kind of highly technical discussion this book seeks to avoid—and knockdown power is strictly a Hollywood stuntman gizmo, there is no such thing in real life, sorry. People shot do not get blown backward through walls and plate glass.

If you really want to get into the reality of the catch phrase *stopping power*, you should look into the IWBA's International Journal of Wound Ballistics, or the FBI's Handgun Wounding Factors and Effectiveness seminar. Or an analysis of blunt and penetrating trauma mechanisms. See, I told you it was complicated. Remember, almost everyone who is shot survives. Shot placement means more than muzzle velocity. English translation: training counts more than hardware.

When you think of handgun *power* (a very technical term), a lot of factors come into play, and as a new gun owner, you should keep these things in mind. The more "power" a gun has, the harder it is to control, the louder it will be, the heavier it generally is, the greater the "kick" or recoil, and the more its ammunition costs. Ammo for any gun comes in higher- and lower-power varieties, which depends on the weight of the bullet and the amount of powder in the casing, so that's a factor too. This is marked on ammo packages, and your dealer can help you with that, try some of each.

As a general (but not absolute) rule, the larger the caliber, the more powerful the gun. (But, for example, a .357 is much more powerful than a .38, part of that absolute insanity of caliber numbers.) Except for macho gorillas, people in general don't like the bone-jarring tooth-rattling pounding of the very-high-caliber high-energy Dirty-Harry-type sidearms (he carried a .44 revolver, far stronger than a .45 semi-auto, go figure). You might try a .44 on for size at a range, as a rental, and then buy something more practical for yourself.

Experts argue endlessly over the best caliber and power for any given purpose, and criticize each other over their choices, but they all agree on these simple facts:

1–One well-placed shot from any gun can be instantly lethal.

2–People have survived shots, even multiple shots, from all types of guns.

3–Stopping power depends more on the person doing the shooting than the gun being used.

4–A gun you can shoot well is more effective than a powerful gun you can't handle properly.

How do I find a good class and trainer?

This is the same problem you have with a dentist, doctor, handyman or anything. You already know the places to look, and their relative quality—phone listings, online search, neighbor referral and what's often best, word-of-mouth.

In this field, a typical source is your local shooting range, where the range itself and the flow of customers tends to weed out the weak and leave the better in place. You look for a while, make a choice more or less blindly, and find out what you've gotten after you get it. Sometimes the best trainers have set up their own schools as entrepreneurs.

Another key resource is the NRA, and don't go getting all political about this. Despite the constant diet from the "news" media, the NRA is the largest gun-safety and gun-training organization in the world, with no one short of armed forces and specialty ops in second place. They are the ones who certify virtually all the trainers (and then there's the military, police, international schools, etc.). Look for your local state association or club and they will be filled with trainers and classes from which you can choose.

A word to the wise—I never met instructors who didn't think they were the cat's pajamas. Their knowledge of guns and ability to shoot may cloud their ability to gauge their teaching and interpersonal skills. It's like a nice lady who loves to quilt and is good at it who opens a quilting store but doesn't know squat about running a business and marketing.

Just like doctors, lawyers, teachers and almost anything else, there are good ones and then there's all the rest. When you've been through a handful, you can sort them by quality. Only the experience of actually doing it puts you in a position of knowing. And that's half the fun of it. Then you can give your advice to the next person who comes along asking this question. And then, instead of telling who's really good, you can tell about who you know, and repeat the cycle.

The Muzzle Test. When you speak with a trainer you're considering, if the trainer handles a firearm, watch the muzzle. If the muzzle points at you, that's not a good sign. If they point the muzzle at themselves, or hold the gun by the muzzle, that's not a good sign. It's also not uncommon. Really really good trainers are rare if this is the test. If they tell you don't worry, it's not loaded, keep looking.

If someone has a gun pointed at me, what good is having a gun anyway?

Not a lot. If someone has the drop on you, having a gun may not matter much. You pretty much figured that out on your own. Cooperate. Pray. Your choices are limited. Facing—or acting—against a drawn gun is *extremely* risky. Deciding to finally get a gun doesn't change that. If you have thought these things through to this point, you have been thinking rationally and are considering the very real problems of surviving criminal confrontations. Good for you. The gun might just give you a fighting chance but it's not a talisman. Are you thinking you're alone, at home, in public, what?

If you're interested, there are advanced books and training on disarming assailants, tactics and strategy for dealing with extreme situations, and perhaps more important, *situational awareness training*, to help keep you from ending up in this predicament in the first place. The highly regarded *Refuse To Be A Victim* program (Google it) focuses on this. The book *The Truth About Self Protection* will open your eyes. While you're at it, look up white, yellow, orange and red states of awareness. What, you want me to do all the work for you? Part of the goal here is motivation, not bottle feeding.

Am I supposed to have a gun in every room?

If you're asking this question you've recognized the problem of *immediacy*. The need for self defense, according to many people who have experienced it, happens when you least expect it, in a way you didn't anticipate it, when you're not ready. If your only gun is in the nightstand but you spend all your time in your study or on the road, well, you don't need me to think this through for you.

"Tactical" issues are very real, and part of a good personal safety plan. Thinking about getting a gun means thinking about staying safe. Despite the difficulties, people protect themselves all the time. There is a lot to learn. Welcome to the school. It is a rewarding education, and it's about time. You're an American. You can do this. Or at least, that's your choice. Books, DVDs, classes, clubs and memberships, the web and chat groups, it is endless and as you'll find out, it is enthralling. The number two participant sport in the country, ahead of golf. I repeat myself, uh, unlike the media.

If I do get a gun, can't the crook just take it and use it against me?

That's a myth the anti-rights people like to spout to scare you away from guns. Maybe it scares them too. But think about that. If it were true, then we could just take guns away from crooks and use it against them, right? It's ridiculous. It doesn't work that way. Sure, a gun can be lost in a struggle, but as a general rule, the person with the gun is in charge. That's how guns work. That's why guns are so valuable. That's why you're thinking about getting a gun. Because you know that if you have a gun, you have a fighting chance.

But isn't the crook stronger, quicker, smarter, better suited, more adept, more likely to get your gun than you are to get his? Think about that too. Think about *mug shots* of crooks you've seen (not movie stars pretending to be crooks). Are those the bright quick-witted people you're worried about? Your gun puts you in control. And you can read up on *gun-retention* and *close-quarters* techniques.

This brings up another key point that's been made and will be made again in this book. A gun works right out of the box. But a gun works better with training. And a gun works better with a whole lot of training. The easiest lowest stress training is with a book, like you're getting right here. That's the First and Second Amendment working together—a free press and the right to arms. Videos are right up there for low-cost easy at-home training.

Next up is class time at a range, private lessons with a friend or instructor, and range time with a friend, instructor, or just by yourself. More is better. But the gun does work right out of the box. It just doesn't work as well, and the risk to you, for using one without knowing a lot about what you're doing goes up. Get trained.

Can I get one for recreation and self defense both?

Any firearm can be used for both of course, but this raises the valid question about multiple guns for multiple uses. When you decide upon Your First Gun you may choose one that is more suited to target practice, or one that is better for a combat situation, or one that can serve both reasonably well. In this book we're primarily looking at sidearms only, which is its own narrow limitation. There is a valid line of thinking that says: "The only purpose of a pistol is to fight your way back to the rifle you should have never laid down." That was Clint Smith, an expert whose writings you should read.

As you learn about the various types of guns and their uses, and how they are suited to your hands and build and budget and needs, you'll make your choice, and like many other Americans, you may find you want several different firearms to serve different purposes. As long as you can afford it, that's fine. We'll stay focused here on Your First Gun. You've got plenty to think about with that.

What does NICS stand for?

NICS is shorthand for NICBCS, the National Instant Criminal Background Check System run by the FBI. It was put in place in 1994 under the Brady bill, to check out the background of anyone who buys a gun at retail from a federally licensed firearm dealer (a gun store). Six-letter acronyms are unpopular so it was unofficially shortened to NICS. The computer itself is in Clarksburg, West Virginia, and it can instantly check out any American from that single location, the true accomplishment of the Brady bill.

All the talk about waiting periods back then, which has since been abandoned, turned out to be just political leverage to get the quarter-billion dollars needed to build this computer and hire the staff to run it. A NICS "instant" background check is conducted before any gun is sold by a federal dealer at retail.

What's the deal with the background check? I've never done anything wrong but the whole FBI thing worries me.

It worries a lot of people, but don't worry, the authorities assure us you have nothing to worry about. When you buy a gun in a gun store, the dealer contacts the FBI, provides your information to them, and they run you through the federal and local criminal information computer systems, and get a quick response in almost all cases. The clerk at the call center (it's actually a contract worker, not an FBI agent) looks at the records and says either: proceed, delay, or deny.

If no contrary information shows up for you, the sale can proceed and you can pay for and get your merchandise. If your name looks like someone else, or if some other glitch raises a flag, the sale can be delayed for up to three business days while the FBI investigates further. If they can't resolve the problem within the three days the sale must by law go through, but many dealers will refuse to do this, afraid of retribution or repercussions against their licenses. If the response is "deny," it means the record suggests you cannot legally make the purchase, and there is an appeals process you can go through. A large number of appeals succeed.

What does "buying off paper" mean?

Since 1968, all regular firearms sold at retail require filling out some federal paperwork, currently a Form 4473 that all licensed dealers provide. It identifies you, the gun you are getting, and info that if answered honestly determines if you are legally able to possess firearms, or are a "prohibited possessor," a person who can't have guns or ammo.

Obviously, there is no lie detector attached to the form, so you could lie, but lying is a serious federal crime. Now, a background "NICS" check is made at the time of purchase, which in theory is supposed to spot all prohibited possessors. It's pretty good but like anything the federal government (or anyone) does, it's not perfect.

The original form stays with the dealers as long as they're in business,* no copies are supposed to be made, and the info the dealers send to the FBI for the check is supposed to be destroyed instantly after it's used. The feds say they destroy it, but there's no way to know for sure and people have doubts. The 4473 form the dealers save is "the paper," and the information the FBI got might be too.

That potential list of gun owners makes a lot of people nervous. A government list of gun owners would be valuable to politicians interested in confiscating guns, and gun confiscation is the very thing that got our Revolutionary War started. I'm not going into balance of power and the political purposes of an armed public here. It is touched upon in the essay section of this book. Lists of gun owners were what enabled disarmament and the genocides of the 20th century.

Now, if you buy or get a gun from your parent, or a friend, a neighbor, or even someone you just happen to meet, which is perfectly legal in most states as we go to press, there is no paperwork and no background check. It is simply the sale of private property between two people in a free society, the same as any other private property, like, say, a book.

And though you might initially think, well, guns are pretty dangerous, well, books are too. They have started wars and revolutions, and governments have decided they should be banned and controlled too, and for good reason, sorta.

Under normal conditions a private gun sale like that harms no one, is not a crime, there is no victim, nothing bad or evil happens and it has been routine for centuries in this nation. You simply end up with your Dad's gun, or your friend's, or a stranger's. And the government has no knowledge of it.**

That's what "off paper" means. If the government had a list of all these it would be a huge and expensive list to keep and maintain, and would serve no crime-fighting purpose, since it would only track the innocent. Owning guns is not a crime.

To many people, off-paper sales have special value, for it truly represents real freedom. For others it scares them, for it truly represents real freedom, and the government has no knowledge of it. This is what the fuss over the so-called gun-show "loophole" frenzy is really all about. It's not about gun shows, and it's not about loopholes. It's about your ability to act completely on your own. It's about freedom. Freedom scares a lot of people. It's about who's in control.

When you read the proposed laws, they typically apply to everyone everywhere—gun shows have little to do with it. The gun-show cry provides political leverage, and video footage the media uses that distorts the issue and instills fear in people with little understanding of the shooting sports.

When a criminal gets a firearm from any source, it's a five-year federal felony. Possessing it after getting it is a federal five-year felony. The transfer is also a five-year crime. That's 15 years of jail time. Criminals get all their guns with no government oversight or paperwork. New laws aimed at new paperwork for you and me won't have any more effect on that than all the existing paperwork laws we have now.

The problems here are not about law. We've passed the laws. It's about *law enforcement*, because the criminals prance around unattended regardless of the laws and background checks the public endures. The judiciary is the other weak link. Bad guys don't get sentenced properly if they're caught.

If you ask about it, you'll hear that the courts are too busy, the dockets would overload, the prisons are too crowded, the cases are pleaded out, and the criminals go through catch and release like fish and are let back out on the street.

The "news" media is a huge part of this problem too because they hide this from you and scream about the need for more laws, which is totally false. When they say we need tougher laws, those will only affect we the people. We need tougher enforcement, and social changes to really deal with the criminal element, but don't hold your breath.

When two low-level operators in the Fast and Furious gun-running scandal were "brought to justice," for supplying 93 rifles to drug lords involved in countless murders, the Justice Dept. gave them each plea deals of one month per gun. One month! This showed just how corrupt the system is. We had all of them—on paper—signed, sealed and delivered.

The Justice Dept. knew the plea deal would shield *the real criminals* from exposure during a trial—and double jeopardy meant we could never squeeze the truth from the perps we caught. They were caught *red handed*, why give them plea deals? Because trials would have revealed government was running the operation—and who gave orders that covered up everything. The "news" media failed to ask about that, but did call for increased paperwork for you and me. Go figure.

* When a dealer goes out of business, federal agents collect all those records, warehouse them, and their exact handling and whereabouts is the subject of some debate and controversy. A centralized registry is against the law, but such registries are known to have been made with similar records.

** The only way to make "universal background checks" work is to list every gun everyone has. Otherwise, the system can't track every sale and who has what. So while politicians may *say* they're only after the "gun-show loophole," they seek an end to off-paper sales. When you read the bills, they call for universal control over every gun owner and every gun, which is why they meet such total resistance from the community. If background checks didn't compile gun-owner lists they wouldn't meet such resistance. A system called BIDS could easily do this—and at only 10% of the cost of NICS. It is described at GunLaws.com.

Should I get a gun "off paper"?

That's a decision for you to make. Just keep in mind that when you get a gun off paper from someone you don't know, you don't know if the gun works. You may not be able to go back after the sale. You also don't know if the gun is stolen or was involved in a crime, and the seller might not know this either—you could innocently, that is, unknowingly buy a firearm with a history (and it could have been bought and sold many times before it made its way to you). Just like anything you might get at a garage sale, *caveat emptor*.

There are serious factors to consider when buying off paper, especially from someone you don't know well. Federal law actually protects you to a certain degree, because the serious crimes require *knowingly* buying contraband stolen property —in other words, deliberately doing something wrong.

If you own an off-paper gun with a "history," and this ever comes to light, it will be confiscated and you'll face some difficulties. Ask around, it's a complex subject. Do not expect any semblance of accuracy or balance from the media if they get involved. They don't understand it and have no desire to treat it in an intelligent way, in my experience. Most private sales are fine. Some folks own some guns on and some guns off paper, so like stocks, they have a diversified collection.

Could you skip all the details and just recommend a gun for a newcomer?

I can, and people will, especially stores that want to sell you something, but you'll be going off half cocked, the perfect phrase for that. It comes from Revolutionary days, when you could have a fully loaded gun that won't fire. Is that what you want? In a free country, you're free to act stupidly, and I don't recommend it. Read the rest of this book before you act, and don't go off half cocked. May I repeat: take a class.

The most general all-purpose one-size-fits-all basic-leather-shoe of a gun is probably the .38 caliber revolver. It's what police carried for decades, they're widely available, highly reliable, good for target practice or self defense, reasonably priced and come in enough sizes to fit almost anyone.

A great choice for a first gun for a beginner is likely a .22 caliber semi-auto pistol. They're fairly easy to handle, with low recoil and not extremely loud (though you need ear and eye protection when practicing with any gun because they're all very loud and can emit hot debris). The ammo is cheap so you can shoot all day long and not break the bank. Because they're lower powered they're easier to be accurate with, but they're potentially as lethal as any other sidearm.

The classic today is the 9mm semi-auto pistol, preferred by most law-enforcement agencies for its reasonable power, good ammunition capacity, ease of reloading and good compromise of the many factors that make for a good self-defense sidearm.

For youngsters, the popular choice has been and remains the bolt-action .22-caliber rifle. The length makes it easiest to keep on target and avoid "muzzle drift," while teaching the elements of sight alignment, trigger control, concentration, proper breathing and practice of the safety rules. A virtual absence of recoil and noise make it ideal for really young people to gain familiarity with the skills needed for enjoyment of the shooting sports.

If you think that's enough to go out and intelligently buy Your First Gun you've missed the whole point of this little book. But you could do it, and people have been buying guns for centuries with less input than even this one Q&A. That's because guns are indeed simple to operate, and can make people of vastly unequal abilities quickly equal in the struggle to survive.

What about all the legal mumbo jumbo?

You'll get the most basic parts of that at the store where you buy Your First Gun, which is why a retail store is a better option than a friend or other private sale for your first purchase. You'll get a product that's legal to own in your state and locale, with proper paperwork, the most essential elements of ownership and possession covered for you.

You do need more than that though, and keep in mind that a gun store's specialty is guns, not law. And you're not dealing with a gun *store*, you're dealing with a gun-store *clerk*, and the clerk's specialty is guns, not laws. The person behind the counter knows about makes and models, prices, how the guns open and close, operate, which ones are better for what uses, things like that. It's a rare clerk, in my experience, who can speak knowledgably about the fine points of gun law (though some are pretty well convinced they know the laws, whether that's true or not).

The next thing you need with Your First Gun—or if you take my advice, *before* you get that gun—is a book on your state's gun laws, so you stay safe, and so the government itself doesn't pose a bigger risk to you than the criminals you may be concerned about.

> *"It doesn't makes sense to own a gun and not know the rules."*

That's been a motto here at Bloomfield Press since we went into business in 1988. Time in prison is a terrible waste for an otherwise law-abiding person who violates some minor infraction that causes no harm but breaks some petty bureaucratic rule. The people in our government who hate guns—and there are a lot of them—have set up such rules.

This is why gun owners have become so upset about the attacks that go on concerning gun rights, attacks that will affect you but have no impact on violent criminals who may have motivated you to make your purchase in the first place.

While some people like to think all the gun laws are infringements on your rights it just ain't so. The laws mete out punishment for criminal acts, and protect behavior that is not a violation of anything, very important principles for the guilty and for the innocent.

At the very least you need to know the rules for the use of deadly force, justifiable self defense, carrying firearms either openly or discretely, where guns are allowed and prohibited, transferring your firearms to others including a spouse, friends or children, traveling with your firearm, legally going shooting outdoors, using your gun in defense without firing (defensive display and threatening to deter a potential crime), it's a long list. Go to GunLaws.com and find a book on your gun laws.

Now it's time to venture out and get Your First Gun.

MY FIRST GUN

"With gun ownership I felt empowered and responsible—I now had the means to protect myself and my family from some of the random evil and chaos of the world. I now had a tool beyond the 911 connection of my cell phone. I also felt in awe of the power in my hands—the power to take a life, G-d forbid.

"Taking gun ownership seriously meant I had to think carefully about ultimate issues. Am I prepared to take a life in defense of my children? My wife? My self? How accessible and ready does my firearm need to be—What is my plan for dealing with it? It meant mandating for myself the physical and psychological training for emergency situations, G-d-forbid, that I truly never want to encounter. It means facing my own mortality and trusting in G-d to protect me and mine." –Rabbi Judah Freeman, Jews for the Preservation of Firearms Ownership

•

"The thrill of ownership was immense for me, coupled with a degree of awe and respect at the power of a 12-gauge shotgun. That was the start, and I progressed into handguns and rifles. Now, as a U.S. citizen, I choose to protect the Second Amendment very seriously." –Chris Bodine, Webmaster

•

"When I was 11, I had saved up enough money doing lawn and garden chores to mail-order a used Remington .22 rifle. My family was surprised when it arrived but didn't object. I used it mostly target shooting and killing rats in the Laurelhurst garbage dump. I still have it, 76 years later, and it's still in good condition. I've accumulated a slew of new and old guns, the oldest a 16th-century Japanese matchlock, along with a lot of other stuff, the stuff of life." –Bobby H.

22 MAKING THE PURCHASE

I've decided to get one, how do I start?

I recommend taking a gun-safety class. That's a big step for a lot of folks, but an easy one, because it's less stress than a diet and less commitment than closing the sale. Beginner classes are often only an evening, and you'll gain exposure to a lot of what you need to know, first hand.

You'll be in a room with others like you where you can listen or share your concerns, or just listen and learn. Classes are available nationwide, but be sure to choose a class for beginners. You don't want a carry-permit class, that's an advanced program for gun owners who already know how to handle guns and shoot well.

You'll have a knowledgeable instructor to introduce you to the basics, and you'll be in the presence of actual firearms, perhaps for the first time, in a safe environment. You can pick them up and see what they feel like—they're heavier than you may think! In some introductory classes you won't even have to fire one, you just explore the safety rules, the types of firearms available, how they work, how to properly hold them and use the sights, and the basic laws that control gun ownership and purchase for where you live.

You'll have an opportunity to get more training, take a more advanced class, look at some firearms available for sale, get a book or video to take home, and decide if you want to take this to the next step. You could even buy one on the spot.

Do be a tad bit wary if a personal friend is into firearms and offers to help, because being a very savvy gun enthusiast and being a suitable instructor for a newcomer are not the same thing. If you're a tenderfoot, a macho introduction to artillery is not what you need, and your friend may not recognize that. Don't laugh, it's been known to occur. A lot. But it's also OK and a time-honored approach.

What's the best place to buy my first gun?

I recommend a federally licensed firearms dealer—a gun store. These are sometimes referred to as an FFL, a federal firearms licensee. The choices include mom-and-pops, big independents, shooting ranges with stores attached, the big-box retailers, chain-store operators, and even private operators working from their homes.

I don't think it's too much different than the purchase of any other retail item. It's nice to get good treatment in a store, but you don't always and it can be unpredictable. The biggest chains can be good or bad depending on the day and the sales clerk you happen to get. A tiny shop can be the best or worst, depending on who runs it and if they have good style. If you make a point of shopping first and returning you can decide if you like the place and the treatment you get before making your purchase. I always shop a lot before deciding on an expensive item, and then go back, but that's me.

By comparison shopping you can check prices for the same merchandise, though you may find it hard to see the exact same firearm in two places. Wherever you make your purchase, that becomes "your gun store" and you will likely go back there with problems you have, or to get questions answered, and for supplies and accessories.

After breaking the ice on Your First Gun, this is where you may hang out a little and learn to talk shop, pick up extra ammo, start becoming acquainted with the gun culture, meet other gun owners and learn more about firearms from a social perspective. So pick a place that seems friendly if you think that will be important to you. The big chains may have the best price and selection, but they can be less personal, or maybe not. American gun stores are still a bastion of family-owned businesses, it depends on what works best for you.

If your circle of friends includes someone who has a gun collection, you might want to buy one from your friend. You can also buy a firearm at a gun show, either from a dealer or from a private party. There are both advantages and disadvantages to this, especially for a first-time purchase, which I discuss in the section about buying guns "off paper." For a first gun, I think a retail sale from a store is your best bet, because you can go back for assistance, repairs, and the reliability factor is important.

What do you think about online gun stores?

They're great once you know what you're doing, but for a first gun, I think a face-to-face transaction is the way to go. The help of another person right in front of you in concluding the sale makes a big difference in making the purchase. You're not looking for anything rare, you'll get a decent price locally, and a local purchase brings you into the community, which I think is important. With an online purchase, you have to go to a licensed dealer at a physical location anyway, to pick up the gun when it is shipped, fill out the paperwork and have the background check completed, so there is little difference from starting at a gun store in the first place.

I'm afraid to even walk into a gun store.

That's natural. Those places can be such testosterone-filled macho man caves it's hard to draw air into your lungs. The sales people want to help but some have little idea how to handle a novice or talk to a woman. Many know almost nothing about women. No, it's worse. Women scare them. Their wives scare them.

You can deal with your discomfort with the best cure for that known on Earth—a friend. This is a perfect use for a friend. Go to a gun store with someone who knows the ropes. That is one of the best things a friend can do, introduce a kindred spirit to a mutual field of interest.

I remember my first gun store. It was in the corner of the Smitty's supermarket in Phoenix. I just stumbled upon it, fresh out of gun-restrictive New York City. You could get a quart of milk, a pound of chopped meat, a gun and ammo. I asked, "What do you need to get a gun?" This was Arizona. The counter guy scrunched up his face, looked at me a little funny and said, "How much money have you got?" I'll never forget it. Neither will you.

Should I buy new or used?

The main value in buying your first gun used is price. You can get a lot more gun for a lot less money if you're willing to buy a gun someone (or several people) have already owned. As a new gun owner with little experience though, this is only reasonable if you buy either from a trusted friend who really knows the ropes and will treat you fairly, or from a reputable dealer.

Guns are built to last, and unless an item has been treated poorly or seen excessive use, a good used gun is a decent option if money is an issue for you. With a little searching you can find used guns with their original packaging and papers, so you get the benefits of a new piece, and it won't cost as much.

New guns come with factory warrantees, but firearms these days are made so well that you typically don't need them. It's nice to buy new, but it isn't essential. It comes down to a matter of personal choice.

What are some of the questions I should ask when I first visit a gun store?

Now there's a really good question. Gun stores love newcomers, but they can overwhelm you. Don't be afraid to tell them to slow down, chill out, take it easy.

"I'm thinking about maybe getting my first gun. Can you help me get started?" If they ask how much are you looking to spend (pretty common) they've already jumped too far ahead, in my opinion. Tell them you're not worried about price. "I need to know what my options are first, I'm just getting started. Show me some common handguns," and you're on your way.

If the salesperson is any good the gun will be *cleared* (opened and inspected to make sure it's unloaded, the first rule of gun safety) and handed to you. Before you take it, ask, "Show me how you did that (cleared it)," and now you start getting an education. If the bozo just handed it to you out of the cabinet, be sure to ask, "Would you show me how to clear that?" If that ticks the person off, you might want to look, hand it back, and move on. I have a very low tolerance for casual gun handling, especially from people who should know better. It's uncommon, but it does occur.

I went into a gun store and couldn't understand all the jargon, so I walked out. I felt miserable, afraid to go back.

Yup, this is a real problem. Especially with a lot of privately owned gun stores, but many of the chains and big outfitters too. It's like a club, and if you don't know the ropes, you're lost. Hey, ski shops and haberdashers can be the same way. They may try to be helpful, but some barely know how.

You may luck into someone helpful, but way too often, you have people who know guns so well, they can't communicate to an ordinary person. They get lost in caliber numbers and slinging lingo at you. It's not you, it's them. The best bet still remains going with a friend who can walk you through, or doing some study on your own ahead of time.

When I go into some completely new field, like a boat show for example, I tell them, I'm completely new to this, so please go easy on me and speak slowly. Then when they just immediately ignore that (they do!), and sling lingo and speak fast, I say it again—please, speak slower and try to use plain English for me, OK? If they can't, I'll exhibit the same courtesy they've shown me, show them my back, and walk to someone else, or out. Then they think I'm the fool, the fools.

Who ever said life was easy. In the end, I'll end up better at all this than they ever dreamed they could be, or think they are. Keep the faith baby. I was in a guitar store like that once. They never saw me again. There are lots of other stores. Their loss. When you find the good ones you have friends for life.

Does brand name matter?

Of course. Some manufacturers are known for high quality, reliability and all the features that make a product top-of-the-line. Other firms make very serviceable goods at far better prices. Still others offer low price and you get what you pay for. Which is better? You certainly want a gun that will go bang when you pull the trigger, so bargain basement, and used guns of unknown character are a risky way to go. Reliability and price are related.

Which brand is which? Ten minutes at the counter of your neighborhood gun shop will answer that some, and you'll be able to eyeball and feel the goods to compare the reputation, and cost and finished product. But a word of caution. Except for the biggest outfitters, gun shops carry only certain brand names, so they will of course pitch the brands they carry, and tend to play down others. That's OK, there will still be a price and quality spread, just keep availability in mind.

Have you found the mind-numbing array of makes and models on the web mind numbing? That's because it is. A handful of names will stand out though. World famous, American-made brands, some of them alive since the Wild West and before, have helped build this country.

Firearms are rich in tradition in America, and owning a brand name associated with these traditions is a point of pride for their owners. There is nothing like owning genuine Colt, Remington, Winchester, Smith and Wesson, Browning, Springfield Armory, Ruger, Mossberg, many others. By the same token, foreign manufacturers produce some of the finest firearms in the world. Glock made in Austria, Beretta from Italy, H&K or Walther with German roots, and others have earned a reputation and market share highly regarded worldwide. It's a matter of taste, looks, style, cost, features and personal choice, just like, dare I say it again, shoes.

What scams should I watch out for on my first purchase?

In a first-rate, brightly lit clean shop with well-dressed staff, not much. They'll try to sell you some accessories, but you need some so that's not really an abuse unless they go way overboard. It's their job to keep revenues up so there is certainly a tendency to walk you into some higher-priced merchandise, but that's fair, expectable and maybe good for you. In my experience, gun people are good people, and I have not run into this sort of problem in this field.

What about guns in colors?

I personally don't go for that, it seems like a marketing gimmick to me, but that's a matter of taste, and it sure seems to work. Guess who buys pink guns. There is an element of style and fashion to the gun business just like any other consumer product, and most guns will never be used in a hostile situation, so if color makes your day, I suppose it doesn't harm anything.

But considering how serious this business is, my own choice and recommendation would be to stay with functional gun-metal blue or black (it reflects less light, making you less of a target and reducing glare which can affect your vision), or matte-finish steel, which is durable and requires little maintenance.

What other stuff do I need with my first gun?

A gun with nothing else is just an awkward club. At the very least you need ammunition that exactly matches the firearm. Here is the bare minimum to be properly armed, all of which you should get when you buy Your First Gun.

Ammunition

Without ammunition a gun is worthless. Ammunition runs out quickly, quicker than you expect.

How much do you need? The standard line is, more than you have. My friend says you should get at least 5,000 rounds for each of your neighbors (in case they run low). You get used to that kind of humor after a while. Yeah, it's pretty wry.

If you enjoy going to the range a lot, you can burn through a lot, which is a good argument for owning a .22, where ammo is sold in boxes of 500 (as opposed to boxes of 50 for most other calibers, but at similar cost). If it's Your First Gun, and you just leave it sit around, a box or two could last years.

A small retail box of ammo has between 20 and 50 individual shots, called *rounds*. Ammo for your gun will be available in many brands and types. I say get one box of each. That may be a lot, but not really in the scheme of things. Try them all out. The differences are subtle, but some may work better in your gun than others. That's especially true for pistols (semi-automatics that use magazines). This will get you enough trigger time to get familiar with Your First Gun, and you'll learn if some ammo doesn't feed well, that is, it jams.

Some types of ammo are cheap and designed for practice. They may have bullet shapes (such as *wad cutters* or *semi wad cutters*) that make nice clean holes in paper targets. Other ammo types can be twice the price or more, and are designed for personal defense. It's important to spend the bucks and shoot a box or two of these also, and see how they perform. They're probably more powerful, which means louder, with more recoil and probably less smoke than cheap training ammo. It's a good thing to know ahead of time.

Talk to the staff and prepare for an earful. There are entire books, no, make that libraries, on the subject, and we're not going into it here. That's why I suggested, get several different kinds that fit your gun and try them out.

All right, just a bare little technical. One single round of ammunition has four main components. The *bullet* is the front part that shoots out of the gun, usually made mostly of lead. It is sometimes coated or jacketed with another metal, often copper, but often just bare lead in a variety of shapes.

The *casing* holds the bullet and other parts and is usually made of brass, but is sometimes made of aluminum or steel.

Inside the casing (also called the *case*) is the *powder* (which has been a chemical other than gunpowder for many years) that burns hot and fast, giving off the gasses that force the bullet down the barrel and out of the gun.

The fourth part is the *primer*, a chemical at the back of the casing, either in a small "cup" in the center of the back (called a *centerfire* round), or around the inner rim of the back of the casing (a *rimfire* round), that explodes when struck by the gun's firing pin, igniting the powder, and firing the gun. A picture is worth a thousand words, and by now you've noticed I've avoided them.

Holster

Carrying a firearm in public, at a range or otherwise is deadly serious business, and a holster must provide fully positive *retention*, meaning your gun can't slip around, or fall out under any normal circumstances. It should fit tightly against your body, which means the belt you use must work with it well. Your regular belts (and your street clothes too) may not be ideally suited to this task.

The holster should be selected for the specific gun it will carry, and experts debate endlessly on the pros and cons of holster design and materials. Some holsters have retention devices such as straps, thumb breaks, finger-release locking devices, fit adjustments and more, which you should review in a good gun store, or books that cover it exhaustively.

Holsters are made for the familiar side hip carry, probably best for you for starters. You'll also find ones for small-of-back, under shoulder, pocket, cross draw, ankle, thigh, and exotic carry like so-called thunderwear and off-body carry.

Now, if you can get past the ignorance on the street and in our mainstream polite society, you'll learn that wearing a gun has a fashion element connected to it as well.

Wait a minute, back up a second. I watch James Bond. I saw Miami Vice. I take that back. Everyone knows tastefully carried firearms are a fashion statement. We're just not supposed to say it in so many words in polite company. Boy does this politically correct stuff get confusing.

Out here in Arizona where I'm writing this, we even have banquets where the invitations include the delicious line, "Tasteful Open Carry Appreciated," and 400 people will show up for prime rib and frivolity, wearing their best leather and gear. It's freedom on a platter, and everyone leaves full, and alive (including the slow waiters).

Getting "fitted" for a holster can be like a session with a dressmaker or haberdasher. One company makes holsters out of exotic animal hides like ostrich, zebra, snake, alligator, and of course, the indispensably rugged rhinoceros.

The varieties are vast and none are perfect. Like shoes, they serve different purposes. Do you want to carry discreetly on your body, openly outdoors or at the range, in a pocket, off body as in a briefcase or handbag? Holsters come in colors and various designs, and in different materials. Leather is classic, nylon and fabrics are popular, hard plastic kydex has advantages, and they all have their advocates and detractors.

Chances are very high that the store that sells you Your First Gun will sell you your first holster from their existing stock. It's also very likely you'll see other types over time and will buy them to try them, and develop a supply somewhere of holsters you have abandoned for others you like more. Happens to all of us.

Cleaning Kit

I get a laugh when I see an old movie where some woman is sitting dutifully cleaning her man's gun with a can of Pledge or something similar and she is making the wooden parts all shiny and nice. Hollywood scriptwriters have heard about cleaning guns but have no clue what it's about. You may not plan on getting yours dirty, but that's OK, guns do that all by themselves, and must be cleaned to operate reliably.

The burning gunpowder from shooting during practice leaves ash inside that can eventually gum up the works. It hasn't actually been real gunpowder for many years, it is something called *smokeless powder* (which isn't really smokeless), or *propellant*. Don't make me get technical on you. Folks just call it powder, and it isn't even an explosive, it just burns, hot and fast, and leaves residue. A basic cleaning kit has the gun oil, residue solvent, brushes, swabs, simple tools, supplies and instructions you need. Keep your gun oiled and clean and it will serve you well.

Eye and Ear Protection

Guns are louder than you can imagine—the loudest thing you will come into contact with in everyday life. Nothing prepares you for how loud they are, not even the loudest rock concert you have ever experienced, which is a distant second, if you have ever been to one of those. You need to wear adequate ear muffs to protect your hearing when you go shooting, so buy a set when you buy your gun, and better yet, buy two sets, so if you go shooting with a friend or family member, you have a set for them to wear.

You can get cheap roll-up foam ear plugs, and they're better than nothing, but get something better and protect your ears. You might consider firing a shot without your hearing protectors to see what it's like. *It will shock you*, and let you know what you face if you ever have a confrontation where you have no time and no ear muffs handy.

I recommend ear muffs with the highest sound-reduction rating, for the greatest protection. You can also get electronic muffs, which allow speech and normal-level sound in, so you can communicate with ease, and automatically shut off low-level sound to keep the roar of gunfire out. Check them out.

Guns also emit burning hot particles and debris, and semi-autos eject scorching hot empty casings which can damage your eyes. It's important to always wear adequate safety glasses when shooting. Ranges do not allow people to use their facilities without wearing eye and ear protection. Often they will provide it, sometimes for a fee. If they catch you without protective gear they may give you a warning. If they catch you twice, you may be asked to leave.

A case designed for transporting a firearm

Transporting firearms goes beyond the scope of this book. In some localities it is illegal to conceal a firearm, in others it is illegal to have it in plain view. Sometimes it must be carried in a particular type of case or securely wrapped, as defined by the laws of the place. Your local store can help you sort out these "traps for the unwary." You'll start to understand why gun owners are upset at all the loopholes that interfere with you and your rights, that have no effect on crime. In any case, you'll need a case for your firearm. If you bought a new gun, it will come in a proper case, save it and use it.

You can buy a case, sometimes called a *gun rug*, of cloth or something similar, with a zipper, or an array of cases for firearms. Always keep guns safely stored to protect them from dirt, rust, abrasion, prying eyes, and so you don't look like a complete rube with a gun in a plastic shopping bag.

Always use proper storage methods and locks when storing firearms at home, work or when traveling, as required by law for your locality, and as your own judgment, safety and prudence require.

MY FIRST GUN

"I grew up shooting and hunting. My Dad had many firearms, but in my 20s I wanted a gun of my own. I'd been reading Jeff Cooper, and after considering a Smith and Wesson Combat Masterpiece (I liked the name but not the .38-caliber) I decided I would get a .45-caliber Colt Government Model 1911. I purchased one in 1976, and I think of it as my Bicentennial Gun.

"The classic Colt appealed to me for multiple reasons. I liked its substantial heft, the smoothness of operation, the crisp trigger, and something more: the heritage. When you've said 'Colt .45' you've said a mouthful. The heritage was important—at that time it dated back more than 60 years. Regardless of the model, I savored its ownership as both a right and a responsibility. It was *my* firearm, for me to enjoy—and perhaps to use—as a responsible adult. Many many firearms later, I still have my Bicentennial Gun." –Billy T.

•

"I started out with a Daisy BB gun, then a Crossman .22-cal pellet pistol, then a Winchester single-shot .22-cal rifle, then a Mossberg 16-guage shotgun, all before the age of 15. I loved them all and learned a lot about life from using them." –Roy Miller

33 Now That You Have One

Once you have decided to take the step, you will one day walk back into your home with Your First Gun, and join the ranks of American homes that are safely armed. Congratulations!

Everything is now different, yet everything is still pretty much the same. You eat your meals same as before, put your pants on one leg at a time, but you now know that your situation is more adult, and your ability to care for yourself has taken a quantum leap forward. A whole new horizon of activity and sport awaits you. A world formerly hidden from your view is suddenly at hand.

So what else do I need besides this book?

A lot. I wrote this book to help you with the *decision* about getting Your First Gun, and the mental attitude and life-style changes that go with it: The maturing and adult-like behaviors and attitudes that go with this quintessentially American household addition.

You'll now need a different kind of first-gun book and education—one that teaches you about *using* Your First Gun: the etiquette, procedures, proper grip, stance and sight alignment. Breath control and trigger squeeze. Target acquisition and the difference between point shooting and use of gun sights.

You need to learn about the laws of your state, and the rules about self defense. If you're serious, take time to learn about tactics, strategy, crime avoidance and the criminal mindset, situational awareness and deterrence. Get exposure to the sporting pursuits (especially plinking, you gotta go plinking) and the hobby aspects of firearm ownership. That includes a world of activity around you from which you've so far been immune—the firearms community, your community—of people living in this peacefully armed world. There is so much more to firearms than the horrifying sliver you've been exposed to every night on TV.

As a gun owner you brush up against an intensely political world. Until now it has been a distant reality colored poorly by a hopelessly biased "news" media. That agenda and spin will get more obvious by the day... they're talking about you.

You might find it prudent to take steps to protect the very rights your are now exercising, expand your political awareness, join a club with like-minded individuals. Do this not only for the camaraderie, fun and training opportunities, but for an ability to stay current on changes to the laws, and even have influence on what goes on. You have a dog in this fight. It's your civil rights now too.

Do I need to register my gun?

This depends on where you live or reside. Your local gun store will fill you in on the details for your location, and will have the paperwork if needed. You'll take care of all that when you make your purchase. If that paper of registration makes you nervous, you'll begin to understand why "infringement" is such a sensitive topic for gun owners.

In a free society you should not have to register yourself to own a firearm any more than you need to register a controversial book, or a Bible, gold, cash, or any private property. It is none of the government's business what its citizens own, in theory at least. Though this may seem counterintuitive at first, there is simply no crime-fighting component to the various gun-registration schemes that are constantly proposed. How does writing down your name, or my name, in some huge government file, make you safer? See the essay, *The Only Question About Registration* at the end of this book for an explanation of how that works.

In a free place like Arizona, where I live, "The Gun-Friendliest State In The Union," there is no registration and no way to register a gun. It is simply private property, you own it, period. You can sell it as you see fit, buy more if you wish, and that's that. The crime rate here is very low, and if you subtract illegal immigrant smuggling and the war on some drugs, we're the proverbial shining city on a hill.

In a city like Chicago, one the most infringed and unfree places in the nation, a sidearm must be registered and re-registered every three years, with paperwork and taxes called "fees" in a massive government-run desk-bound bureaucracy. If you fail to re-register *each* of your guns *every* time, and keep paying the tax, they can never be registered again and permanently become contraband. How that helps prevent crime is never explained, because it can't be explained. Chicago has enormous problems with gangs who are armed to the teeth, murder each other day and night, and never register their guns. No surprise there.

What about carry permits?

I don't recommend this for newcomers, not in the sense of going about town armed, certainly not at first. Some new gun owners think they need a carry permit to go with their new gun—and in some jurisdictions you may need some sort of "papers" just to possess the gun. That might include provisions for carrying it, or even to bring it home with you, you'll find out locally.

The red tape can be burdensome—in Washington, D.C. it takes months and can cost more than the gun. But that's different than what's typically called a CCW permit (Carry a Concealed Weapon permit) for walking around armed. It goes by a lot of other alphabet-soup names and acronyms (CHL, CWP, CWL, CCL, CCWP, CCHP, FOID Card, etc.)

You need a whole lot of training and familiarity with Your First Gun, in my opinion, before you're ready to even consider having it ready and out on the street with you. C'mon, you know that. An understanding of shoot/no shoot scenarios is in the way-advanced-class for a newcomer. Your First Gun may not even be well suited to tactical carry, and you won't learn about concealment techniques and proper draw from concealment for a while yet, so I'd say put this out of your mind for now.

That said, your right to defend your life at any time and place should not diminish based on training or skill. However, your exposure to legal risks and other dangers go up, the less training you have. When you think about it, it's a disgrace that public schools keep students so ignorant of the realities surrounding Second Amendment activity.

A big mistake fostered by government-run concealed-firearm programs is that those classes are all wrong for new gun owners. You need gun-training 101, to learn proper shooting stance, sight alignment, grip, breath control and the like. You need to gain confidence with the gun you have, how it works right down to its parts, and learn to shoot it effectively and at various distances. Ideally, you should go through hundreds of rounds of ammo in practice, to become a good shot, not the handful of rounds that a permit class requires to qualify for the "right-to-carry" permission slip.

If, after you have gained comfortable confidence in the use of Your First Gun you feel it is time to take a next step, then a carry permit may be right for you. You may also, by that time, have gained enough political awareness to understand the hypocrisy of carry permits, and the idea that government licensing your rights with taxes, computer lists, fingerprints and expiration dates is fundamentally wrong.

If that happens, the bright appeal of Constitutional Carry may make more sense to you, and you may want to go to a state where your rights are intact, or become more politically active and press your state to move in the direction of more freedom. Read about this at GunLaws.com.

How can I go to the range for practice without breaking some law?

We haven't covered much law in this book, and as a responsible adult you do need to become acquainted with the laws for the state and place where you live. **You can get a good start on what you need to know about your gun laws at GunLaws.com.** It's sad to say that government has made this far more complicated than it ought to be or than it used to be. Each state has different gun laws and some are far better than others. On top of that, federal gun laws apply in all 50 states, but that provides something of a safety valve (because some of those laws protect you, as well as serious infringements we won't go into in this book; for more on that read *Gun Laws of America*).

Under federal law, it is legal to transport a firearm from one place where it is legal to have, to any other place in the country where it is legal to have, if it is unloaded and separate from ammunition, in the trunk of a car. If you're in a vehicle without a trunk, like a pickup truck, it should be in a locked compartment not accessible from the passenger compartment.

Now that's a general statement, it isn't legal advice, and there are exceptions. That law is called the Federal Firearms Transportation Guarantee, it was passed as part of FOPA, the Firearm Owner's Protection Act in 1986, federal law number 18 USC §926A.

In a disgraceful refusal to obey the law, some repressive states have ignored this federal law and arrested innocent people who are legally traveling with a firearm. What that means is the government poses a greater risk to you than some crook, and it is a very real crook itself (and a terrible situation in a free country like ours). A crook might take your money. Government will take your freedom and your money, and scar your record for life.

New York, New Jersey, Massachusetts, Washington, D.C., Maryland, and California are among the worst offenders of your civil rights in this regard, so be especially cautious if you are traveling there. One of the main principles is this: do not get stopped when you are traveling with a firearm.

Obtaining a carry permit for simply transporting your firearm is often considered wise, since most authorities recognize it and let gun owners pass unmolested. Yet only a few percent of gun owners get carry permits, which require being fingerprinted and recorded in the government criminal database, along with the taxes, tests, papers, delays, photos, qualifying and expiration dates. It may provide expedience, but is a serious deterrent to many—a high price to pay for exercise of a basic civil and human right.

Ask for advice at the store where you obtain Your First Gun about transporting it, and then be extra cautious, especially at first. Don't speed, signal your lane changes, don't do anything that will lead to a roadside stop, and you will avoid this most embarrassing and potentially difficult situation. You don't normally get stopped right? That won't change once you are a law-abiding gun owner. But you *might* get nervous if you're stopped while armed and understand the noise gun owners make about police intrusion into privacy.

How often should I practice?

World-class pianist Vladimir Horowitz reportedly once said, "If I don't practice for a day, I know it. If I don't practice for two days, my wife knows it. If I don't practice for three days, the world knows it." Olympic gold-medalist shotgunner Kim Rhode reportedly went through $700 worth of shotgun shells *per day* in the run up to her record-setting performance in the 2012 London games. So that's the top end of the chart.

On the lower end, way too many police officers fire the minimum number of rounds a year (between 30 and 50 in some departments) needed to keep their certification as sworn officers. I've heard that occasionally an officer ends up embarrassed at the range to find the duty gun rusted shut in the holster from weather and sweat.

On the civilian side, some people buy a gun, never shoot it, put it in the night stand unloaded, and die at home of old age, which is probably not a bad strategy if you can manage it. I'd recommend something in between.

Hopefully you've at least tried the gun you obtained, so you know it works, and if you like it or not, and if you can handle it OK. Now get used to it, familiar with it, get yourself accustomed to it. When it becomes second nature, like an old friend, something you can rely upon, and not have to think about it too hard, it will serve you far better in an emergency. And maybe that is how much practice you need.

You want to be able to pick up the thing in the dark, make sure it's loaded and ready to fire, and operate it under stress if needed. How much practice do *you* need to do that? Guns are designed to be operated by an idiot under stress, so that lowers the bar a little.

Professionals will advise a ton of practice, and people who are dedicated to this practice constantly. A subscription to a firearms publication, or membership in a club will set you on a path toward practice and ongoing education.

If the hobby and sport grabs, you won't need encouragement to get to the range and bust some caps, burn some powder, get that freedom smell in your nose and blood-pumping excitement in your veins. I also know for sure that many of you will show some level of enthusiasm at first, and then that will wane over time. It's entirely up to you. At least make a point of going out during 4th of July National Training Week and dusting off the ole shootin' irons.

Do I have to get my gun modified?

If you're dealing with Your First Gun you don't need to worry about this very much. All sorts of modifications can be made by a competent gunsmith, but a good model as supplied by the manufacturer is more than enough for learning and gaining proficiency for a long time before you go seeking changes. Why spend money on tricking out a gun before you learn to shoot it accurately and reliably first.

Typical modifications for a sidearm include changing the grips—which come in a huge variety of shapes, sizes, styles, materials and colors, replacing the front and rear sights, having the trigger mechanism adjusted in different ways, adding attachments to the muzzle... you can easily double the cost of a firearm by adding and changing its components. You'll find thick catalogs filled with options. Don't worry about any of that just yet. Chalk it up to a new hobby, if you want to go down that road.

What do I tell my kids about my gun?

Rather than give you a partial answer to this very important question, I'm going to suggest you read the short booklet, *Gun-Proof Your Children* by the world-renowned expert Massad Ayoob. That's what I did for my daughter and I believe it was the right choice. It also has pictures this book doesn't. You've started on a journey of discovery and can't get all the answers from this one short book of mine. Decide right now to get all the education you and your family need.

Should I buy my child a gun?

This book isn't going to cover this issue. Parents who know what they're doing, who are comfortable around guns and have used them as adults, make the decision to introduce their kids to firearms when they feel their children are ready. This is a time-honored tradition, which often begins with family or parent-child time at the shooting range, slingshots and BB guns in the backyard and similar outdoor pursuits.

When the time is right, youngsters get their first gun, perhaps a bolt-action junior-size rifle or a small-bore shotgun, or some other firearm appropriate for children. Some time after you get and become familiar with *your* first gun, you'll know when it's right to answer this question for yourself and your family.

Depending on the gun you chose for yourself, and the age of your child, it may be too powerful for your child to handle. Little kids, and small adults in general, should be introduced to lower-powered firearms at first, so they don't get their socks knocked off and end up turned off to the world of firearms before they have a chance to appreciate it.

I have friends over who drink and know nothing about guns, what if they found mine?

You know the answer to that. Don't let it happen. Don't bring up the subject. Make sure your firearm is safely stored where it cannot be found either by accident or if deliberately sought. Keep it locked away, and keep exclusive control over the access to it. You haven't needed it on poker or football night or whatever so far, and you will not need it now, so leave it that way. Be smart. Don't be in the evening news.

Should I let my friends know I have a gun?

This depends entirely on who your friends are. You might want to broach the subject gently with one at first, if you are really unsure. In a general social setting you could ask what they think about people who own guns, especially with all the news about more and more people buying guns. Quietly listen to their responses. Change the subject if it becomes overtly hostile or argumentative.

Are you so far outside the "gun culture" that your friends look down on gun ownership? Do they stereotype and frown upon people they don't know who own firearms, or make disparaging remarks when they hear about people who own guns? Do they equate stories about criminals who misuse guns, with citizens who own guns? Do your friends literally hate guns, and hate gun owners, as many people do—and then, surprise—think they believe it's not good to hate? Well then, of course you might not want to tell them. And you might start thinking long and hard about who your friends are.

If you tell a circle of people like that you are thinking about getting a gun (don't tell them you have one, they may freak out) they may turn red and ostracize you and literally cast you out. Your decision about this may set you apart. Ponder the prospect, it is significant. Are these friends you want? Or want to lose? Are the values you have held all along the values you still want to retain? Can you reconcile the differences, or just let them slide, how big a change is this?

Firearm ownership is a litmus test. It is for politicians, and I suppose, for friendships. The independence, willingness to cleave to a traditional set of values, stand up to prejudices, hold to what you believe is right in the midst of adversity, it is a measure of character, and a dividing line. You may not have considered it this deeply, but firearms are a way of holding actual freedom in your hands. This may be as important a part of your decision as anything. Give it the thought it requires.

You may be pleasantly surprised. Your friends may already own guns and are simply quiet about it, as many people are. You may learn that people you have known for years are gun owners and just never discussed it with you before, sensing you were not open to the subject. They may welcome you into the community with open arms. A whole new world of friendships and camaraderie may await you.

Now all you need is a tactful and subtle way to approach the subject, if that's what's called for. You could mention that publicly traded firearm stocks are doing well (or not) and see how a person reacts. When a self-defense story appears in the news (they're common in real life but rare in the "news," bring it up; for stats on how bad reporting is on this, read *The Bias Against Guns*) and raise the subject. On my site, GunLaws.com, the news-media-accuracy button will rock you with stories of media deception that keep the public uninformed and fuel the gun debate with misinformation.

Should I let anyone see or play with my gun?

See? Maybe. Play? Of course not. Read the rest of this book, take some classes, read some more books, watch some training videos, go to the range with Your First Gun, and get enough understanding so you can answer that question yourself. Sharing guns at the range? Now *that's* fun.

Do I keep my magazines loaded?

One of the generic rules of *gun safety* is to always keep guns unloaded until ready for use. One of the generic rules for *self defense safety* is, a gun that is "safe" isn't good for anything. Loaded magazines fall somewhere between these two rules.

At the front of this book you saw the widely recognized rules for gun safety—*the rules for making sure guns do not shoot when you do not want them to.*

These perhaps need to be balanced with the so-called Lovejoy's *rules for making sure guns work when you need them* for their designed purpose—to protect people.

Lovejoy's Rules of Gunfighting Safety

1. You must have a gun.

2. Your gun should always be loaded and ready to fire.

3. The first hit counts more than the first shot.

This gets into some of the heavy-duty realities of surviving criminal encounters, a subject you, as a new gun owner, only have a passing acquaintance with—and most of that is of the fairytale variety from pop culture. Hopefully it points you toward Phase II of this whole exercise—learning about self defense, *pistolcraft*, and the field of marksmanship, a great American tradition and a valuable modern social skill. From that standpoint, you never have enough loaded magazines.

But I digress. If you've decided to keep a lot of spare magazines there is no need to keep them all loaded, but really no reason not to. It's a personal choice. I've heard it said a magazine's springs will "fatigue" if left compressed for a long time by being fully loaded, and then won't properly feed ammo, but I haven't found anything to support that. At a range, people have bags full of magazines stuffed with ammo and they generally work fine, though magazine springs do give out after years of use. I'll tell you, media types who complain about magazines or having too much ammo have never been to a decent range.

How many magazines should I buy?

The standard joke is you never have enough. Most new semi-auto sidearms come with two, and you need at least one for the gun to work properly (you can get some but not all semi-autos to fire a single shot by manually placing one round in its chamber without a magazine).

When you're at the range practicing it's nice to have a half dozen or so for each gun, so you don't spend all your time reloading, and here's a tip you won't get from watching TV. You spend more time loading than shooting when you're at the range! That's an argument for having lots of magazines. And that comes down to a simple matter of money and storage space. When the zombies attack, well, you never have enough.

What do you think of the NRA, really? Why do they have to get involved and make everything so political? Don't they just lie about everything?

So what do you think, is the NRA the feared and much-hated powerful gun lobby? Or is the NRA America's oldest, most respected, and largest civil-rights group in the world? Which version do you get from the nightly "news"? Does the unbiased "news" at least present a little of both? Hmmm.

Wherever you stand on this controversial question as you contemplate Your First Gun, you won't be able to escape this, despite the total media blackout:

The NRA is the most comprehensive gun-safety and marksmanship-training organization on the planet and has been for more than a century.

You knew that, right? It is responsible for the basic safety rules everyone uses, and the underlying firearm-training principles police, military and civilians have relied upon since such things were first organized. It has trained tens of millions of individuals and hundreds of thousands of instructors in the safe, proper and legal use of firearms for all legal purposes since just after the Civil War. The media taught me that. Not.

If you get firearms training it will undoubtedly be from NRA-certified trainers because they're the ones who study, develop the programs and do it, for the nation and ultimately the world. You can stay as far out of the politics of having your guns as you like, and abandon the NRA in their perpetual struggle to protect your rights as many people do, and they will still be there training the trainers, and providing the thinking that makes gun use among the safest pursuits of anything you can do in modern times.

Can't I just fire a warning shot to scare off a bad guy and not have to shoot anyone?

If you're wondering about this, and who wouldn't, it shows how badly you need to come up to speed on the self-defense laws. That's a subject this book barely goes near.

There is no legal justification for firing a warning shot. None.

That means you cannot legally do it. Despite all the nonsense you see about this on TV and in movies, if you do this, the cops will turn all their attention to you, not the bad guy. Didn't I tell you that everything you see in the media about guns is baloney?

You can be charged with all sorts of crimes for doing this. Because warning shots are dangerous to bystanders (even a mile away when the bullet comes down) they are a very bad idea, and causing injury or damage in the process, even by "accident" could be a felony and lock you away for years.

The legal rights you have to shoot in self defense or in resisting certain crimes do not in any way allow using a firearm as an "audible warning device," and it will attract all the attention to you (since the bad guys will have long since split). Your firearm will be subject to confiscation, and you really don't want to explain your innocence to uniformed officers at your door, smoking gun in hand.

If the situation isn't immediately life or death, don't fire. If you really are locked in mortal combat, don't waste a potentially life-saving shot making scary noises. Firing a warning may serve as evidence that you didn't believe the situation presented an immediately deadly threat, and so you really did fire without justification. Don't give prosecutors that wedge.

A warning shot is an irresponsible fool's tool of Hollywood ignoramii (who constantly promote this dangerous crime), that has little place in the real world. If you shoot and miss, that's one thing (and a missed shot is dangerous of course).

If you shoot *intending* to miss, that's just reckless discharge of a firearm in a place where shooing isn't allowed (like in town, or alongside a road), and there will be repercussions. "I was just trying to scare someone away without hurting them," won't cut it. And that sounds suspiciously like making a statement to a responding officer without your lawyer present, pal.

What's not in this book that I need to know as a new gun owner?

If you read the segment just above this one you can sure guess at that answer. Plenty. Start by reading the book, *After You Shoot: Your gun's hot, the perp's not, now what?*

A few things in this little book bear repeating, and I have. This book is designed to help you with the *decision* you face in getting Your First Gun, as a person who has lived without one for your entire life, confronted with an endless barrage of myths, misinformation and distance from the subject. By now you have either decided that gun ownership is not for you, or that it is time to join the community of Americans who keep and bear arms. Now you have to *learn the ropes*.

The best single piece of advice I can give you is to take a class. A face-to-face program will give you more experience and personal understanding than anything else I can recommend, even if the instructor you get is not the finest on the planet. It's like Zen and the art of motorcycle repair. You can read all you want about changing the oil on a bike, but until you actually do it, well, you get the point. If you have a fear, face it, deal with it, learn, then decide.

Next up is reading, but then, I'm a writer, so what do I know, and I'm not exactly an unbiased observer. Would that there was a single book I could recommend, and in this book I have recommended many. Scan the back of this book, and make a selection that seems right to you. Some are specific, some are general, they aim at different people. Get a whole bunch and dive in. Try a video. Try the *Armed Response* gunfight simulator DVD on your TV, there's an experience.

In terms of subjects you need to cover, let me reiterate that one of the best things about a gun is that it works right out of the box, so even without knowing almost anything, you can pick one up (just like in the movies, they did get this point right), load it, and at close range in the most desperate emergency, use it to save your life. The chances of that occurring are near zero, but it's good to know that once you become a firearm owner, that level of safety is at hand.

That said, you do need to know how to load it, which means you do need to know how to open it, and ask for and buy the right ammunition, and it helps to know how the sights work, *and listen to me now:*

Do not load Your First Gun in the house until you take it to a range and have someone knowledgeable show you how Your First Gun works.

When you get Your First Gun, the person who provides it should show you it is completely unloaded. You should personally confirm this in the cylinder, the chamber and the magazine. Make sure you know what that means and that they are truly empty. The magazine, if any, should be removed, and know how to lock back the slide. Man, they should not let you out of school without a rudimentary understanding of this sort of thing.

What exactly do I do when I get home?

Physically working the mechanism and handling the gun should only be done at a shooting range with a competent individual supervising you, until you become competent yourself. You've already decided upon storage in your home, put your prized possession there until you can get to a range. Go about your business. You will feel your gun's presence in the house, that's natural.

Only with scrupulous care does the firearms community maintain its exceptional safety record, and you are now responsible for maintaining this record, for your own safety and for the rest of us. As rapidly as possible, you should learn how the physical parts of your firearm work, so you can open, close and manipulate the parts with smooth ease and confidence.

Let's say you already know how to work the mechanism and can clear the gun and prove it is unloaded. You're going to want to look at it.

Read the safety rules at the front of this book again. Go ahead, I'll wait.

Keeping your finger off the trigger, and with the muzzle pointed at something you'd be willing to destroy if the gun went off, which you have thought about and identified in advance, out of sight of the neighbors so you don't create a panic, and with your ammunition in a completely different physical location than your firearm, you can *visually* inspect your firearm to gain familiarity with it.

The ultimate gun-safety procedures would require you to avoid even this level of contact, but it is hard to imagine you are not going to look at your gun once you get it, if you already know how it works. If you don't know how it works, you are going to leave it sit until you do. It's like owning a car before you know how to drive. It sits. But you can look.

Next comes the practical steps of going to the range. You'll need a certain amount of gear simply to go there and not look like some rube. You can carry your firearm and ammo in a plastic shopping bag, but even the greenest tenderfoot can tell that's going to look pretty lameass. Don't waste money on slick gear but do get some. The store that sold you the gun, or a local gun show, or a friend's closet can get you started, and you'll quickly figure out what else you need, or want. You can shop till you drop in this hobby.

I love watching the old cowboy Westerns, where if the hero is looking at you dead in the eye he can nail you from a block away, while holding the gun at hip level. Man, it does *not* work that way! When you're at a suitable range try it. You won't even hit the paper, let alone the bull's-eye. You *need* the sights.

Do you know which is your *dominant eye*? Find an object on a distant wall. Now make an "OK" sign with your thumb and forefinger and look at the object through the opening with both eyes open and your arm outstretched. Now draw your arm toward your face and it ends up in front of one eye, your dominant one, which plays a role in aiming. But I digress.

There is *so* much more. You're entering an exciting world with magnetic appeal, which is why the shooting sports are the number two participant sport, second only to exercise.

You may be content to make sure your gun works once, at the range, or outdoors if you're lucky enough to have enough land, and then leave it in the nightstand for the rest of your life (not recommended). Or you may find out a lot of your friends go to the range more often than they run marathons, and you'll be joining them. Whatever it turns out to be for you, welcome aboard this wonderful American pursuit.

So now do I have to get into the gun debate?

No. But you might be sorely tempted to. As a gun owner, or as a person thinking about getting a firearm, you'll have what to say when the subject comes up. Be careful. And for Pete's sake, leave talk about your own gun, or lack of one, out of it, at least at first. Trust me on that.

You might do best to just avoid the subject of guns at least for a while, especially with friends whose opinions you're not sure of. People can get awfully riled up over this subject.

There are so many pitfalls, rumors that seem real, myths that seem like facts, statistics that are made up, traps for the unwary, verbal landmines everywhere—you might just want to listen and observe instead. You'll learn more that way, and stay out of embarrassing no-win situations. My Dad taught me, "When you're talking you're not learning." Good advice, Dad. Don't lose any friends in a debate that's best left alone.

MY FIRST GUN

"I probably had a lot of toy guns as a kid but the only one I remember was my Daisy BB gun. The first real gun I had was when I went into the Army. In basic training we were taught how to handle a real rifle—a British Enfield bolt action. It was not to be called a gun but our piece. The first day we went to the range I was scared stiff. I had never fired a real rifle before and I didn't know what to expect. I trembled as I squeezed off the first shot. After that it was easy. I eventually fired expert with a carbine. I also eventually qualified with the .45 caliber pistol, the grease gun, and managed to get some time on the .50-caliber water-cooled machine gun, now *that* was a gun." –Irving Korwin

•

"My first gun was an Ithaca single-shot .22 rifle. It's sitting in my safe now waiting for another small person to come into my life. I received the little Ithaca on my seventh birthday. I only got to shoot the .22 under the hawk-like supervision of my Dad. First he would load for me, but eventually he would hand me each round which I carefully loaded. With the gun ready to go, he would talk me through the process of shooting.

"'Take a big breath... Let half of it out... Are your sights on the target? Squeeze the trigger a little more every time the front sight gets on the target... Crack! 'Good shot!' Smile. On my eighth birthday, I received a Daisy BB gun which I was free to carry and shoot independently in the big vacant field behind our house.

"Even though I was relatively free with the BB gun, on the range with real guns, I still received each round individually until some two years later. We were at an informal gravel-pit range with friends. Dad had given me a round and I had taken a shot. As I waited for him to give me the next round, he slid the box over to me and gestured toward it. It was a graduation moment. Years later I asked him if he remembered it as a significant moment. He remembered, but had not realized what the moment meant to me. It just seemed to him that I had shown sufficient responsibility to manage my own loading.

"Shooting and gun lore were integral to my relationship with my Dad. It was a focal point that grew into a shared passion. I miss him mightily, but have a great legacy built around simple lessons in safety, responsibility, and the skills of shooting." – Author Chris Knox

•

"I received my first gun at age 16. My father bought it for me. It was a Stevens 16-gauge single-shot shotgun with an external hammer that had to be cocked before each shot. My Dad thinks he paid $50 for it. A few years ago I loaned it to one of my nephews, so it is still somewhere in the family." –Attorney James Marovich

•

"My father's brother, an amateur photographer, had been in the tank corps that liberated some of the German concentration camps during World War II, and documented what he saw. During my boyhood he shared these photos with me. The most shocking of these were the piles of emaciated bodies stacked up awaiting the ovens. My uncle emphasized that the Jewish people were disarmed by their own government and their victimization had been significantly facilitated by coercive gun-control laws that effectively outlawed their self-defense. He also showed us firearms that were 'bring-backs' from that war. One of them was an American rifle, an old bolt-action Springfield. I remember thinking it was very heavy.

"After moving to Colorado for college, I was invited to join a bear hunt in the high country. A friend offered to loan me a rifle—it turned out to be the same kind of Springfield my uncle showed me many years before. As I felt the weight of it in my hands, the horrific images of the concentration camps returned. I didn't get a bear on that hunting trip, but I did get a renewed sense of the importance of firearms ownership. On my return, I began shopping for something I could call my own. I could not afford much, so I settled on an old double-barreled shotgun, but there was no doubt in my mind what it meant to have my own firearm. What I held in my hands was not a guarantee, but a powerful vote in my own destiny." –Author Charly Gullett

•

"I didn't own my first gun until I was 40. I bought it in the aftermath of the death of a beloved family pet from terminal organ failure, the drawn-out and painful final throes of which my wife and I discovered we had no way of easing other than by loving but ineffectual presence. The crisis was on a Friday evening, with no professionals available for more than two days. A well-placed gunshot would have been the only merciful resolution to her agonized suffering.

"That night I vowed I'd never be caught short in such a situation again, and decided to purchase a handgun. My wife and I settled on a simple Browning Buckmark .22, which was selling for $263. At the time, I was a member of Handgun Control (now the Brady Campaign) for over seven years. I was not an anti-gun person. I had enjoyed BB rifle shooting as a youngster, and took pistol classes in college PE. This was not inconsistent—I believed HCI when they told me they merely wanted to keep guns out of the 'wrong hands.' I believed gun ownership was perfectly fine for responsible adults with clean criminal records who wanted to own guns, and I believed HCI when they told me this was their stance as well.

"I was a well-established, middle-aged, home-owning, taxpaying family man with no police encounters other than a few traffic tickets spanning 25 years. I hadn't been in a physical altercation since grade school. I was a graduate of MIT, had an unblemished credit history and employment record, a professional technical career, and held extremely sensitive clearances. I was a Boy Scout volunteer, rarely touch alcohol, have never had any mental health or legal troubles and was on good terms with my neighbors, as were my wife and kids. And, since it still 'counts' to officials in many areas of the country, let me add that I'm even white. In short, next to me, Ward Cleaver came off like Charles Manson.

"Unfortunately for me, I was a resident of Massachusetts. When I discovered all the incredible hoops, hurdles, political and personal influence that was necessary in my area to complete this simple transaction—not to mention the six-month wait!—I came to realize that if 'responsible' people like me were having trouble exercising a guaranteed constitutional right, then something was very, very dangerously wrong with my local government, and any government boasting the same kinds of laws. Especially when it was a lead-pipe cinch that one person I knew could get me any type pistol I wanted, no questions asked, within a week; and that probably any criminal in the state could say the same.

"I finally came to the conclusion that my core belief that a responsible, adult American citizen should always have the ability to own arms for defense of himself and others was incompatible with the gun controllers' true aims, regardless of their protests to the contrary. The Brady Campaign had been lying to me.

"I am currently a member of the NRA (ironically, a legal requirement for handgun ownership in Massachusetts) and a certified firearms instructor. I regularly inform others how the benefits of gun ownership far outweigh the downside. I have found that once people understand what I understand, they are likely to reject the gun-control position, or at least be much more skeptical of it. I still own the Browning, to which I added an inexpensive red-dot scope a few years ago in deference to my aging eyes." –C.D. Tavares

44 ESSAYS

The Only Question About Gun Registration

Dear Editor,

Only one thing is overlooked in the common-sense proposals to register guns, so here it is. How exactly would writing down my name, or your name, help arrest criminals or make you safer? Although at first blush, gun listing has a sort of tantalizing appeal, on reflection you have to wonder whether gun lists would be an instrument of crime control at all.

The unfortunate answer is that, no matter how good it feels when the words first pass your ears, registering honest gun owners doesn't stop criminals, and in fact focuses in exactly the opposite direction. It is an allocation of resources that has no chance of achieving its goal, if that goal is the reduction of crime.

1. Registering 100 million Americans is extremely expensive.

Do you know what it takes to run a database that big? You'll need 27,000 changes *daily*, just to keep up with people who move once every ten years on average. That means floor after floor of cubicle after cubicle for employees with permanent jobs, payroll, parking and dry cleaning bills. It's a government jobs program all by itself, all in the common sense—but deceptive name—of stopping crime. How many criminals do you figure will register when all is said and done? That's right, none, and the planners know that. All that money and time, invested on tracking the innocent! That's why so many police departments are against it— they'll be forced to run huge data centers with their limited resources, and hire clerks instead of cops.

2. Americans who fail to register would become felons without committing a crime.

Under registration, activity that is a common practice and has been perfectly legal since the nation was founded— simple gun ownership—would make you a criminal for failing to fill out a form. Think about that. Possession of private property would subject you to felony arrest, if the property isn't on the government's master list. Boy, that doesn't sound like the American way. No other evil is needed, there is no victim and no inherent criminal act takes place. Paperwork equals prison. That's just wrong.

3. Registration, if enacted, will create an underground market for unregistered guns bigger than the drug trade.

How many times must an elite forbid what the public wants, before learning the unintended consequences of outlawing liberties? People get what they want either way, it's just a question of how much crime the government itself forces to accompany it. With respect to guns, the last thing you want to encourage is the creative import programs and price supports that drug dealers enjoy, for gun runners.

4. People have said to me, "But Alan, if all guns were registered and there was a crime, then you could tell."

Tell what? If your neighbor is shot, that's not probable cause to search everyone with a matching caliber in a ten-mile radius. The factors needed to conclusively link a person to a crime have no connection at all to a registration plan—you need motive, opportunity and means, then witnesses, physical evidence, the murder weapon itself. Your ownership of a gun doesn't make you the person who used it. Police aren't waiting for official lists so they can start catching murderers. Gun registration schemes lack a crime prevention component. Canada abandoned their federal feel-good list scheme—at the insistence of their police forces—after wasting $2 billion on it, that could have gone instead into fighting crime.

5. You don't really think authorities would use gun registration lists to confiscate weapons from people, do you?

Despite real-life examples recently of exactly that in New York, California and Louisiana, and global history for the past century, this couldn't really happen, do you think? Who would even support such a thing in a country like America, with its Bill of Rights? The guarantees against confiscating property, unwarranted seizures and the right to keep and bear arms would surely forestall any such abuse of power, right? There aren't really U.S. politician who would support firearm seizures, are there? OK, sarcasm off. Unfortunately, it's a long list of "officials" who wish to use registration lists to disarm the public.

And what about a simple First Amendment test? If it's OK for arms it must pass muster for words too, OK? Why would an honest writer object to being on some simple government list of approved writers? Why indeed. Let me answer this rhetorical question for you, since reporters I know have a hard time with it. It's because, if you published a story or an editorial and you weren't on the list, you'd be subject to arrest. That's why. That's why government registration for your freedoms is totally unacceptable in a free society.

Pile logic on logic, and some people still just feel the government should register everything, just to keep control. When government has that much control, you no longer possess your liberties. You're living where government lists define who can do what, and where people control trumps crime control—the gun-control model precisely. This form of "gun control" isn't about guns, it's about control.

I might favor registration if the system would include criminals. In fact, I'd favor testing the system on them first, which is only reasonable. But the U.S. Supreme Court, in a widely known case (*Haynes v. U.S.*, 1968), had determined that a felon who has a gun cannot be compelled to complete such forms, because it violates the Fifth Amendment right against self incrimination. That's right, mandatory registration—not in your case of course but in the case of a criminal—is a self-indictment of a crime, and is therefore prohibited.*

Gun listing is a feel-good deception that passes unquestioned by the "news" media, engorges the federal or state bureaucracy, and undercuts the linchpins of American freedoms. It has no more place in a free society than a government authorized list of words or approved writers, and should be rejected outright. Elected officials who promote such a scheme are opposing the very Constitution they take an oath to preserve, protect and defend, and deserve to be removed from office.

Sincerely, Alan Korwin, Author
Gun Laws of America

* NOTE: The *Haynes* case only concerned a limited class of weapons, "destructive devices," which are listed and tracked in a special federal registry under the National Firearms Act. Congress rewrote that law after *Haynes* to require only the legal transferor to file papers, and not the transferee receiving the item, and along with other clever changes this overcame the 5th Amendment problem. In *U.S. v. Freed*, 1971, the Court agreed the problem had been fixed (for possession of hand grenades by criminals in that particular case).

A general registration scheme would run into a greater problem. A criminal can't have a firearm at all, so mere possession of a gun is a serious crime. An additional charge for failing to register the gun (that can't be legally possessed in the first place) would offend the 5th Amendment the same as in *Haynes*, so registration would have to omit criminals, the supposed goal of registration schemes.

However, possession of an unregistered gun by an ordinary citizen would turn that citizen into a felon, with no other illegal act but the paperwork failure. The innocent would then have to register to remain legal, while the illegal possessor could not register without violating the right to not incriminate yourself. The whole thing is a boondoggle that increases the size and power of government, while doing nothing to make you safer or control crime. If this got confusing, it's only because it is, so don't blame me, blame the people trying to foist it on the nation.

MY FIRST GUN

"We lived 15 miles east of San Diego in the 1950s. I was a good kid—energetic, studious and responsible. I got my first real gun, a bolt action Remington .22 rifle with a tubular magazine when I was 9 or 10. Dad and Mom gave me two rules: 'Never point it at people and always assume it's loaded.' Dad and I would drive deep into the countryside for target practice about once a month. He would sit in the car and read a book while I fired at tin cans. I realize now that my love for my Remington blended with the larger experience of bonding with my father. When I had a problem I would interrupt him while he was reading. 'Got a minute, Dad?' and he would put down his book. 'For you, son, I have all the time in the world.'

"My parents knew I would be good. I would have to answer to them, and loved them too much to misbehave. I would also have to answer to our neighbors. I respected all adults, especially my teachers—I could never let them down. There were also the folks at church and the minister who made friendly house calls. All these expectations—within a tight social ecosystem—made me a fully accountable boy and created the exhilarating freedom for me to own a real rifle. And there was one more item that allowed me to be a very young gun owner: if I ever did anything wrong, I would ultimately have to answer to God." –Jon Haupt

•

"I don't actually remember *my* first gun, as I was surrounded by guns and shooting from my earliest memories. Dad hunted to feed us while working the farm and going to college. He managed to find time to compete locally as well. I think the first gun that was actually mine was a .30-cal carbine, but I still cherish that old Model 70. There are so many that are so good and memorable how can one pick?" –Geoff Beneze

•

"My first firearm was a Stevens single-shot .22 when I was six years-old. It was my great grandmother's. She lived to be 102 years old and told me stories of using it when she was a kid in 1906. I carried that rifle with me every day in the woods of northern Minnesota when I was six and seven years old. That rifle represented adventure, independence and responsibility for me. It's not worth much but it is one of my most treasured possessions." –Darren LaSorte, NRA-ILA Manager of Hunting Policy

"In my first real post-college job in 1967, I had folks wearing bed sheets shooting at my co-workers and harassing me—until I bought a gun and waved it at them. Merely because I was white, had Missouri license plates on my vehicle and was helping Negroes (time-warp term) gain *equal opportunity*. Yes, I was an 'outside agitator' to them. People like me had been killed just three years earlier. That taught me what firearms meant, and I have understood that ever since." –Joseph E. Olson

"Although I've handled many weapons in the Army, I never bought a firearm of my own until long after my service. When my eldest son planned on going to Israel for a six-week program, I decided to teach him about firearms and got a nice AR-15 locally, the civilian version of what the Israeli Army issues. In the unlikely event he was in the midst of a terrorist attack, and a wounded Israeli soldier's rifle was available for my son to use, I wanted him to be able to pick it up and fight back to protect himself and his friends. I could not bear the thought that he might die at the hands of some terrorist because I had not taught him how to use a firearm.

"I priced out various models, bought it brand new (and probably overpaid a bit for what I got), but got good support at the store. I taught my son how to safely handle it, disassemble and assemble it, clean it, clear jams, load it, and shoot it. I did the same for my second son and plan on doing this with my daughter as well. It gives me great peace of mind knowing I did everything I could to give them a better chance to survive a terrorist attack during their visit to Israel. Knowing we have this capability at home is of equal value." –Howard Levine

•

I got my first gun during the riots that swept many cities in 1968. I was a young father living off a main artery leading out of Wash., DC. Police told the radio news they weren't certain they could contain the rioters, and they might be moving into the suburbs along the highways. I lived right off one of those. I had had almost no contact with guns, but I decided that with a shotgun I would not need training to hit something -- or many attackers if that were the case. I went to a sporting-goods store and bought a Remington 700 semi-auto and a box of ammo. That was before the federal Gun Control Act, and it was years before I fired it or got any training, but it never committed a crime or caused any harm, and I've learned a whole lot since then. –Larry Pratt, Executive Director, Gun Owners of America

•

"Brooklyn, late 1940s, I was a young Jewish school boy with a compelling, distracting interest in fishing, guns and hunting. I read all the outdoor magazines I could get—*Outdoor Life, Sports Afield, True*—I was a first generation American preoccupied with the great outdoors. When I discovered I had a cousin in Maine, the primeval forest of the North, I hatched a plan. I saved money I earned delivering orders for the fruit store, and dreamed of my first gun.

"My pals thought me crazy, parents weren't enthused, but when school let out for summer, with an OK from my folks I visited my cousin Murray in Portland to go 'fishing,' in the wild waters of the North. With meager gear I took the Greyhound and Murray's wife met me in Portland. They thought I was there to fish, which was true, and we did, and I caught my first pickerel—I was officially a member of the outdoor community. But I had an ulterior motive.

"I located the local hardware store and at first opportunity I went and bought my first gun! I had read, dreamed and planned and knew exactly what I wanted. A gleaming brand new Daisy pump-action BB gun. I will never forget the excitement of that moment. Finally a gun, a rifle, in my hands. I read every word of the manual and tirelessly worked that wonderful action. Rubbed it with oil, lubricated all moving parts and shot it again and again, one little tube of BBs after another. I sighted it in and the die was cast. Sadly, I was not allowed to bring it back to Brooklyn, and although I intended to go back one day and retrieve it, I never did.

"That was a long time ago and in the intervening years I didn't fulfill my dream of joining Mossad, but I did hunt Africa and almost every other continent. And all because of a boy's fantasies come true with the aid of many a boy's first gun, one made by Daisy. Another Daisy hangs in my home now, to plink at cans and bring back those fond memories of long ago.

"That little rifle and my time in the outdoor world taught me a few lessons I have carried with me all these years. Little things like basic gun safety, treating and handling a gun as if it is always loaded; knowing that the real safety is in your head; knowing a gun, even a BB gun, is not a toy; and understanding respect for others and the property of others. Those are the lessons of gun ownership." –Bill Berlat

The Role of Firearms in the Preservation of Peace and Freedom

Introduction

There is scant research on "the role of firearms in the preservation of peace and freedom," a required subject for the Arizona High School Gun Safety Program, where I live.

The following curriculum material takes the form of a textbook chapter, to acquaint both the teacher and the student with the complex role the use of force plays as both an enabler of and threat to personal and national peace and freedom.

Throughout history, the struggle for state and individual sovereignty and peace is the story of the use of force. The most sophisticated and effective tools available in each time period have been taken up in the pursuit of both aggression and defense, conquest and resistance, crime and crime deterrence, and have been equally wielded by the guilty and the innocent.

War making and defensive planning have evolved and continue to do so. Civilization has progressed from rocks and clubs, to walls and battering rams. The metal ages gave us swords, lances and armor. Ingenuity brought us from the bow and arrow to the crossbow and catapult. Technology and oriental wisdom brought us gunpowder, the ability to defend or attack at great distances, and the heart of the Arizona Gun Safety Program.

The struggle to use the power of tools to preserve freedom or take it away is not likely to go away, given the present nature of humanity. This eternal struggle is summed up by the Cooper Conundrum, discussed in the next section.

Part 1: What Is Peace?

"You can't separate peace from freedom because no one can be at peace unless he has his freedom."
–Malcolm X, Speech, New York City, 1965

"You can have peace. Or you can have freedom. Don't ever count on having both at once." –Lazarus Long, in *Time Enough For Love*, by Robert Heinlein, 1973

"Liberty means responsibility. That is why most men dread it." –George Bernard Shaw, 1856-1950

"The concept of peace ranks among the most controversial in our time. Peace undoubtedly carries a positive connotation; almost nobody admits to opposing peace; world peace is widely seen as one of the most noble goals of humanity. Various groups, however, differ sharply about what peace entails, how best to achieve it, and even if peace is truly possible." wikipedia.org/wiki/Peace

The Cooper Conundrum

Col. Jeff Cooper is generally considered "the father of the modern technique of shooting." Prior to his research and the training programs he developed from it, people were taught to shoot sidearms with one hand. Even police officers would practice with one hand behind their backs and a single hand on the firearm. (Long guns, due to weight, center of gravity, and the leverage caused by their length, cannot be effectively fired with one hand with any consistent degree of accuracy— they are two-handed devices by their nature).

Today, a two-handed grip is widely accepted as the correct basic way to safely and accurately handle a sidearm, due to Cooper's pioneering work. Training and qualification in sidearm proficiency will often include practice in strong- and weak-hand techniques, since in emergencies these may be necessary. Under normal conditions however, Cooper's two-handed approach is the way the modern world turns.

In his classic short book, *The Principles of Personal Defense*, Cooper begins by observing that, "Some people prey upon other people. Whether we like it or not, this is one of the facts of life... the peril of physical assault does exist, and it exists everywhere and at all times."

Wish as we may there is no end in sight to this unhappy condition, the Cooper Conundrum, the main reason lasting peace is so elusive. For this reason, the innocent must, if they are to be spared the injustice of homicide, theft or enslavement, be prepared to defend themselves against other people who would take what is not theirs to take, including innocent life. Preserving your personal peace and freedom requires the use of force. People can do it themselves, or organize or hire others to do it for them.

The Concept and Principles of Self Defense

No one is legally obligated to defend against an assault, but everyone has legal protection to do so. You are free to put up no resistance to an attack, and perish, if you so choose. Some religious teachings endorse praying for your attacker as you are slain.

However, legal recognition of a right to self defense goes back as far as recorded law exists, to the Code of Hamurabai, in 1750 B.C. In the United States, legal recognition of the right to defend yourself (or loved ones or other innocents) against an illegal assault goes back to before the signing of the Declaration of Independence.

Whatever method is employed to provide this protection for an individual or for the entire population—police, military, militia, civil, mercenary, personal or other—the protection can be seen as necessary for the good of society.

Until the nature of the human condition changes, peace will require some form of strength to resist aggression, if life and property have value. Moral arguments are made that you actually have a duty to protect your own life because it is precious, and to protect the life of your family members and even other innocents if you are able.

People bent on aggression, on preying upon their fellow citizens, on bringing death and destruction against their neighbors, naturally seek the best means at their disposal to accomplish their evil, or at least aggressive goals. They may be mean, angry, greedy, wicked, deranged or just hungry, but this is not to say they are stupid. It is in their best interests to use the most effective, powerful and lethal tools they can obtain to attain their ends. They understand this instinctively, and arm themselves accordingly.

So we arrive at the fundamental paradox of peace on planet Earth: *The most deadly and effective tools that can be used to stage an attack are the same ones defenders need to protect themselves.* Whatever improvements either side can muster, the other side must quickly adopt. The sword, in classic terms, is double-edged. Gunfire operates in both directions.

[NOTE: Specific issues of personal self defense are outside the scope of this class. The laws involving use of force are complex, subject to change, and class instructors are not generally qualified to discuss personal use-of-force issues with competence. Use-of-force questions that may arise in this segment of the curriculum should be referred to qualified legal advisors and certified trainers. Teachers must resist the temptation to enter into dialog about how to act during a criminal confrontation, or to discuss hypothetical or actual cases of assault and defense.]

Utopia And The Role Of Force In Preserving Peace

In the days before gunpowder, castles and moats provided effective defense against many forms of attack. In terms of preserving peace and relative freedom within the walls, a properly constructed fortress kept out those who would prey on the people inside. This model worked well and lasted for centuries.

The invention of gunpowder ended that. Cannon fire could reach inside, and breach the walls no matter how carefully constructed. Invention of the long bow defeated the defense provided by armor. The crossbow was such a major advancement it was the nuclear weapon of its age, considered improper for use in civilized warfare. The Iron Age supplanted weaponry made of wood and stone. Defenses against those who would prey on others continually migrate forward to new tools and tactics, while evil keeps a watchful eye.

In humanity's interminable struggle for the peace of personal safety, an evolution of defensive technology inexorably advances.

The gradually escalating balance of power is humanity's quest for peace as well as the very bane of its existence. It may seem ugly, or counterintuitive, but it accurately describes what has taken place over the full course of human history. Of all the definitions of peace, the practical ones recognize a need to preserve peace. This preservation only comes through the use of, or ability to threaten the use of, force. This is generally called *peace through strength*. The modern U.S. Marines frame it a little more bluntly, as, "peace through superior firepower."

Utopian notions of peace recognize a possibility of peace without force, and without even the potential to threaten force, in a world of true enlightenment and enduring tranquility, abundance and prosperity. This of course requires a fundamental shift in human nature across the planet, and does not appear likely any time soon. When people who pray completely supplant people who prey, we might arrive. The Cooper Conundrum must evaporate before utopian ideals can be realized.

For utopian peace to arrive, we need a world without the four horsemen of human havoc—where no one is angry, hungry, stupid or wicked. A world where no one takes your stuff by force—even by "legitimate" taxation—to give to someone else. Even if modern technology holds the promise to eliminate hunger (and it's not clear that it does—or that the will exists to do so), no means for alleviating the other three human traits (angry, stupid, wicked) is known, all of which conspire to deny true lasting peace for us all.

Other Ideas About Peace

A more practical approach presumes that peace is not an end place or destination humanity will arrive at "some day," but that peace always exists in varying degrees at various times. It is not static and immutable, a thing that exists only in some complete uncompromised way. Peace exists now, to some extent, and is partially conditioned on how you personally choose to view it.

In his controversial and thought-provoking book, *Report From Iron Mountain on the Possibility and Desirability of Peace*, author Leonard C. Lewin proposes that peace is neither attainable nor desirable. Cleverly presented as a secretly leaked government research document, it addressed subjects that might have been summarily dismissed if released in another fashion.

He argues that the true nature of war is not the advancement of political goals, but economic in nature. The degree of adjustment that would have to take place to achieve a true condition of peace—absence of war and the machinery for making war in all its forms—would require a retooling of economies larger than anything ever attempted, and a collapse of the nation-state system that no one really wants.

Lasting peace would not be in the best interests of a stable society, Lewin posits, because armies are actually indispensable social welfare systems, needed to manage certain elements of the population. The perpetual threat of war is the fundamental organizing force behind government and the ultimate reason for people's adherence to its rule. Spending vast sums of money on war readiness is only remotely related to defense—it is the only flywheel of sufficient size, that can be adjusted arbitrarily at political will, to balance a nation's economy. In that sense, it mimics certain precepts of Marxism. Yes, controversial.

The need for arms to ensure peace has a lot to do with peoples' intent, and personal intent does not easily submit itself to management. It has been said that if the Arabs surrounding Israel laid down their arms, there would be peace, but if the Israelis laid down their arms, there would be no more Israel.

On a smaller scale, "keeping the peace" in the modern world typically falls to a police force of some sort—government agents specifically tasked with monitoring the public and attending to problems that arise. Police are by their nature a coercive force that limits freedom. They do this, in a free society, with the willing cooperation of the majority of the public. In repressive societies they do so typically against the will of the people. Whether they rely primarily on social pressure or actual force depends on many factors.

In more turbulent societies, or those with higher numbers of sociopaths, police are armed. For this purpose, historically, police are provided with the very latest arms, yet frequently they complain that criminals (who of course cannot legally have any weapons) are more numerous or better armed than the police are. Once again, criminals may be mean or evil, but they are not stupid.

This last point is a crucial one. In an effort to preserve domestic peace and tranquility, societies all outlaw possession of any sort of arms by criminals, but this doesn't have the desired effect. Criminals arm themselves because— that's what they do. Laws fail to prevent it, and at best, can only penalize a small number of neer-do-wells, and only if and after they are caught. Even under the most repressive regimes, those who would resist or fight against the social order take up arms, despite any laws to the contrary.

The havoc criminals and other internal anti-social individuals play on the peacefulness of a nation is not abated by law, and though the amount of havoc is in some poorly understood way affected by social programs, poverty, living conditions, culture and numerous other factors, it is only countered directly by the use of force.

Part 2: What Is Freedom?

"Freedom is participation in power" –Cicero

"The enemies of freedom do not argue. They shout and they shoot." –Dean Inge (1954)

"It is criminal to teach a man not to defend himself when he is the constant victim of brutal attacks." –Malcolm X (1964)

"The natural progress of things is for liberty to yield and government to gain ground." –Thomas Jefferson

In a classical sense, as the Founders approached it, freedom is the ability to do as you please of your own free will, as long as you do not harm others. The proper role of government then is primarily to preserve freedom for those governed. Government derives its just powers from the consent of the governed. It may sound pretty basic today, but these were radical concepts when first introduced.

Freedom is not universally recognized as a desirable condition. Under socialism and other totalitarian models, the desire or need to manage the public and achieve stated goals conflicts directly with the idea of free choice, individual liberty, and freedom for society as a whole.

Until the invention of consent of the governed at the formation of the United States, the idea of personal freedom barely existed, let alone enjoyed status as the most highly desirable living conditions a person could aspire to. People were typically subjects, ruled by their betters, mere peons who existed at the whim and will of the king or other autocrat. Classical Greece and Rome moved beyond such repressive models, but only for a privileged elite.

Even today, many people distrust freedom, and prefer central constraints that to some extent remove uncertainty and provide for "the common good." To the extent that a perceived good conflicts with a person's freedom to act without coercion, freedom is compromised. Clearly, a state of pure freedom is unachievable in a population of any size.

A natural tension exists between the concepts of peace and freedom. To preserve peace, and help ensure freedoms of every description, people of their own accord form governments. Examples of people living in any sizeable communities without governance of some form are essentially non-existent.

Yet government rule depends upon coercion and force, and limits freedom. Government has been defined in many ways. Author, businessman and libertarian candidate for President Harry Browne, in his seminal book, *How I Found Freedom In An Unfree World* defines government effectively for the purpose here—government is a way for one group of people to impose its will on another group of people.

Whether for good or bad (however you might care to define those terms), people, through government, decide how things ought to be, and then enforce those decisions on everyone through rule making (laws), and enforcement techniques (primarily police and courts).

Even under basically democratic principles, where each person has a say in how things will be, the freedom to act— for everyone in the system—is constrained by the laws created. Your freedom is limited by the very institution established to protect it.

A single Mountain Man, living in the fenceless expanses of the American West of the 1830s, was probably about as close to free as the world has ever seen. He could holler, make fires, dig holes, dam up a stream, do anything he pleased, and there were no rules or constraints placed on his actions, other than the immutable laws of physics and nature.

In the modern world, with the needs and presence of countless other people impinging upon us in every moment of our existence, even while we sit at home alone, pure freedom is an illusion.

Perhaps one of the greatest freedoms remaining in this country is freedom to travel. Yes, strict rules, fines and prison terms control access to a driver's license, possession of a vehicle, and use of public roads. But from within the framework society has deemed appropriate, a person can travel to most any spot, at any time, as often as desired, with no need for schedules, permits, permission, prior planning or anything but the means to do so. You can buy all the gas you want and go. The freedom of the road tugs at the wanderlust in us all.

The Weaponless World and Balancing Power

Because most freedoms are maintained and implemented through the use of force on those around us, a lasting condition of real peace (weaponless, utopian, flowery total absence of war or the ability to exert force) apparently cannot exist while we enjoy any measure of freedom.

A magical world where weapons cease to exist—where by a wave of a wand America is suddenly gun-free—does not get us any closer to peace or freedom. In fact, it makes matters worse. The good guys, it turns out, need to be able to protect their freedoms.

Contemporary images of a gun-free America may envision an entirely disarmed public, but do not go so far as to imagine an entirely disarmed state—the police, the military and officials remain armed in such scenarios. Even in the hoplophobic fantasies of the most ardent anti-gun-rights advocates, police are armed to protect us from criminals who do not disappear with an imaginary gun evaporation.

Somewhere deep inside, the idea of solving problems of peace and freedom by simply eliminating weapons, nags. How would that work? The fascists, the radicals, the hardened criminals, religious zealots, sociopaths and psychopaths, would-be dictators and tyrants—they do not become peaceful or go away merely because we disarm and make ourselves defenseless.

Instinctively we recognize this. Strategically, people charged with protecting freedom understand this. In fact, the problems supposedly solved by blanket disarmament get worse, since we can pretty much rely on bad actors picking up clubs, or knives, or enough machine tools to start making guns again.

So the gun-free-society model generally presupposes a heavily armed government presence—drug enforcement agents, secret service, air marshals, border patrol, customs officers, coast guard, postal inspectors, and of course, local sheriffs and police. Not to mention a National Guard and armed forces of Army, Navy, Air Force and Marines. Plus private detectives and some bodyguards. And maybe even a militia (a subject covered in the history of the Second Amendment portion of this class).

Would American society be the bastion of freedom, the linchpin of liberty on the entire face of the Earth, if the government was armed to the teeth and the public was completely disarmed? It is such a massive change from the way this country has always been, it is difficult to imagine the scope and effect of the change. The hopeful do dream of a world where hostility ends when government is fully in control at last. The skeptics aren't so sure.

How would "the proper authorities" treat the populace, knowing the people were defenseless, and that all coercive power was concentrated in their own hands? Were the Founders correct about the deterrent effect of an armed populace? Officer Friendly might not change one bit. Or maybe he would. Or maybe he would over time. Or maybe his evil twin, Officer Bullybully, would give vent to some darker motivations. Police, it should be noted, have a higher incidence of domestic violence than almost any other demographic group. Some people exhibit very little trust of police in their communities, borne out of hard experience.

We can look at one such population that was indeed completely disarmed by force of government, with all power held in official hands, and it is not a pretty picture. It is the picture of slavery in early America.

Possession of a weapon by a slave was unthinkable and outlawed, with the death penalty for violations. It is easy to see that, had slaves been able to take up arms, there would be no way to keep them slaves. Placing the power of force in their hands would have set them free just as surely as denying it to them helped keep them locked in bondage.

It is possession of the means to enforce your freedom that foils oppression, while it simultaneously compromises peace, in a delicate balance with no ideal resolution.

Genocide and Democide

History has made clear that genocide, that horrible desecration of all things humane, is perpetrated by the very governments ostensibly in charge of peoples' security. In practically every case, genocide is preceded by government-enforced disarmaments of the public—the intended victims. (Check jpfo.org for horrific details; their video, *Innocents Betrayed*, graphically portrays the sordid history of government-sponsored genocides of the 20th Century and is a recommended adjunct to this course).

Tyrants realize, and little argument need be made, that a government bent on murdering a portion of its citizens can do so easiest if the citizens are first disarmed and rendered helpless. That's why they all take that step.

It turns out that the greatest killers of human beings are their own governments, a phenomenon known as *democide*. Democide, and genocide (the attempted extermination of an entire race or identifiable group of people), were responsible for 262 million deaths last century alone (Notre Dame Law Review, *Is Resisting Genocide a Human Right*, Vol. 81, No. 4, May 2006, Kopel, Gallant and Eisen, citing UN and other sources).

With such a shocking number as a base, it's hard to imagine how any increase in civilian deaths that might result from expanding private gun ownership (such as increased crime, acts of anger, accidental discharges, recklessness, negligence, etc.), could be a problem of similar scale. In net, millions upon millions of lives would be saved, if genocidal regimes faced a noncompliant populace.

Some observers attribute the fact that the awesomely powerful and pervasive U.S. government has basically never turned on its own people, to the high percentage of citizens who keep and bear arms. The Founders repeatedly stated this as a primary purpose for establishing an armed citizenry—as a deterrent to tyranny. Based on the record, it seems to have worked. (This is a complex and intricate analysis that requires comparisons with other nations, none of which are in the world-leadership position of power that the United States is, and is beyond the scope of this program.)

Domestic examples where the powerless were oppressed, such as blacks living in the southern states, and labor riots in the early 1900s, are indeed examples where the people did not own arms to defend themselves. Many of the roots of civilian disarmament, what is often referred to as "gun control," are well known and well documented acts of racism. (See, for example, *Gun Control and the Constitution*, edited by Robert J. Cottrol, Garland Publishing, NY.)

Although it will likely always remain a subject of debate, this is why it is said that, "Guns are why America is still free." The natural tension between freedom and peace is an unfortunate fact of life, and not about to end.

Part 3: A Gun-Free World

It's easy to picture a gun-free world. Just go back in time to before guns, and look at history. You find a more violent, less stable and less safe world than we enjoy today. In a gun-free world, instead of stick-up men, gang bangers, Al Capone, Josef Stalin and Mao Tse-Dung, you have highwaymen, Attila the Hun, Genghis Khan and Julius Caesar. They wiped out entire civilizations, and raped, pillaged and plundered, with impunity, without guns. It was times like those when you really needed a gun. Or two. And a whole lot more ammunition than whatever you had.

Eliminating guns merely shifts the balance of power to the strong and the brutish. It does not eliminate the Four Horseman of Sociopathology—Angry, Hungry, Stupid and Wicked. And it does not provide peace or enhance personal or national freedom. Until those horsemen are somehow defeated (and no one has even a remote idea on how to do that) the good guys need their guns. For safety. For protection. For deterrence. For the children.

If guns suddenly disappeared by magic, the good guys would have to reinvent them, and quickly. It wouldn't be hard— Communist China, Brazil, Italy, Russia and other high-quality gun-producing nations we have little control over would simply flood the market with product (with prices shifting as supply and demand move with market changes). Well-intentioned desires to disarm America typically overlook and would do nothing to stop weapon production abroad. (In fact, our own Army currently relies on the Italian Berretta for all its sidearms).

Import restrictions would have roughly the same effect on guns as they do on illegal drugs and immigrant workers, namely nothing. If you like the war on drugs, you're going to love the war on guns.

Pragmatic plans to eliminate guns, or types of guns, focus on the innocent, by enacting laws to ban or severely restrict legal possession. These ignore the criminal element, who are armed and remain armed despite countless laws passed to stop them.

In an irrational dash to "stop the violence" and "make you safe," well meaning but misguided efforts attack property owned by honest people, who haven't done anything wrong, and leave the status quo for bad actors. Such efforts may seem clever, or feel good, but are reckless, dangerous, and expose decent people to enormous risk. Disarming an innocent person is an act of violence.

You can wish it wasn't so, but peace and freedom depend on a balance of power and the threat and use of force, in this best of all possible worlds.

The people who would enslave you, rob you of your freedoms, and take what's yours, including your life, are held at bay by brute, naked force, and nothing else yet devised will do the job.

America is armed to the teeth, and remains the freest nation on the planet, a magnet to people everywhere. Few people are running to escape from America, because it's the best place to be. Guns save lives. Guns stop crime. Guns are good. And guns are why America is still free.

"People sleep peaceably in their beds at night only because rough men stand ready to do violence on their behalf." – George Orwell

NOTES
1. Moral arguments exist to suggest that although there is no *legal* duty to defend yourself, you have a *moral* duty to protect yourself, your loved ones, and even other innocents, based on the sanctity of life, and a duty to remain available to your family. Personal survival at the expense of an aggressor. The moral argument also exists to practice a utopian form of pacifism, forgo defense of yourself or anyone else, offer no resistance, and perish in the face of a lethal attack. Pray for your enemy as he slays you. Legally or forcibly requiring either approach would be generally seen as amoral. The decision is up to the individual.

2. *Hoplophobia*, n. Irrational, morbid fear of guns (coined by Col. Jeff Cooper, from the Greek *hoplites*, weapon. May cause sweating, faintness, discomfort, sleeplessness, rapid pulse, hypertension, nausea, more, at mere thought of guns. A significant portion of the opposition to the right to keep and bear arms is related to this poorly understood medical condition, yet is often erroneously attributed to matters of law, legislation, precedent, custom, history, and other rational matters.

Hoplophobes are common and often self-involved in attempting to set gun policies. Because arms are fundamental to the preservation of peace and freedom, hoplophobic behavior is potentially quite dangerous, threatening the innocent with defenselessness. When confronted, hoplophobes typically go into denial, a common characteristic of the affliction. Often helped by training, or by coaching at a range, a process known to psychiatry as desensitization, useful in treating many types of phobias. People suffering from hoplophobia deserve sympathy, and should seek treatment as much as, for example, hyperactive children need medication.

3. The actual percentage is disputed, and because gun ownership has existed since the nation's founding and is essentially a private matter, the percentage of armed households is not known with certainty. Estimates place it as low as 25% and as high as 50% or more. One widely quoted statistic suggests that 72 million American homes have at least one gun, which would be 65% of the nation's estimated 110 million households. Some states are believed to have higher rates of ownership than others (in Montana, it is jokingly said that everyone has a gun except for a few crackpots).

New retail gun sales, easily tallied due to the federal background check required under the Brady bill, were running between 8–10 million per year, but many of these are known to be to people who already own firearms, or could represent no sale, multiple firearm sales or were for other purposes than sales. Statistics compiled by SAAMI, The Sporting Arms and Ammunition Manufacturers' Institute (saami.org), indicate that Americans purchase between 5–9 billion rounds of ammunition each year.

When compared to crime statistics, this indicates that, though largely unreported, 99.98% of all gun activity in the country is for legal purposes (0.0002, or two ten-thousandths of gun activity is illegal and subject to punishment). Since inception in 1998, the NICS system has completed more than 140 million background checks, with 16 million in 2011 alone. This reflects the scope of this sector of the civilian economy, largely unreported and generally hidden from public view.

About Alan Korwin

Alan Korwin, author of six books and co-author of eight others, is a full-time freelance writer, consultant and businessman with a twenty-five-year track record. He is a founder and two-term past president of the Arizona Book Publishing Association, which has presented him with its Visionary Leadership award, named in his honor, the Korwin Award. He has received national awards for his publicity work as a member of the Society for Technical Communication, and is a past board member of the Arizona chapter of the Society of Professional Journalists.

Mr. Korwin wrote the business plan that raised $5 million in venture capital and launched the in-flight catalog *SkyMall;* he did the publicity for Pulitzer Prize cartoonist Steve Benson's fourth book; working with American Express, he wrote the strategic plan that defined their worldwide telecommunications strategy for the 1990s; and he had a hand in developing ASPED, Arizona's economic strategic plan. Korwin's writing appears nationally regularly.

Korwin turned his first book, *The Arizona Gun Owner's Guide,* into a self-published best-seller, now in its 25th edition. With his wife Cheryl he operates Bloomfield Press, which has grown into the largest publisher and distributor of gun-law books in the country. Built around ten books he has written on the subject, it includes the unabridged federal guides *Gun Laws of America* and *Supreme Court Gun Cases,* a line of more than 250 books, buttons and DVDs, and more than 1,000 radio and TV appearances. He was an invited guest at the U.S. Supreme Court for oral argument in *D.C. v. Heller,* which led to his 11th book, *The Heller Case: Gun Rights Affirmed.* His 12th book, on the limits of free speech, *Bomb Jokes at Airports,* was followed by *After You Shoot: Your gun's hot. The perp's not. Now what?* His 14th book, in 2013, is *Your First Gun.*

Alan Korwin is originally from New York City, where his clients included IBM, AT&T, NYNEX and others, many with real names. He is a pretty good guitarist and singer, with a penchant for parody (his current band is The Cartridge Family). In 1986, finally married, he moved to the Valley of the Sun. It was a joyful and successful move.

Bloomfield Press is the largest publisher and distributor of gun-law books in the country. These products are mentioned in this book or are good choices for newcomers. Check out more than 250 items on our website, GunLaws.com. Knowledge is power—stay safe.

EMERGENCY PLANNING

It's a Disaster! Bill & Janet Liebsch. 284 p., #IAD $14.95. *The book Dept. of Homeland Security uses,* available by special arrangement. Not like other manuals, this is organized by disaster *type*—flood, storm, hazmat, heat and cold, wildfire, disease, terrorism, radiation, evacuation, more, covering each in great detail. Includes a full first-aid section for multiple needs, public contact numbers, attractive two-color format. Ask us about large quantity discounts.

FIREARM FREEDOM IN NOVELS

Alongside Night. J. Neil Schulman, 302 p., #AN $19.95. Among the finest libertarian novels ever. Government predictably collapsing, underground battles with a ruthless FBI, massive shift in economics reshaping the nation. A brilliant young boy and his mysterious girlfriend (who carries a silenced pistol) struggle to free the boy's father, who can save America. Reignites a sense of liberty that has been dulled by infringements we endure daily. Uplifting.

We Hold These Truths. Skip Coryell, 328 p., #WHT $9.95. Small-town America drawn into stopping a Muslim terrorist with suitcase nukes. The FBI is on it, but it's a preacher who teaches marksmanship, a local newspaper editor who has found the value of firearms, and good people in the town who battle the islamist. A geopolitical redneck thriller, MidEast meets MidWest. Brings back the value and duty of armed citizens.

SELF DEFENSE DVDs
See the full selection of videos at GunLaws.com

Armed Response 1: Fundamental of Defensive Shooting. #D-AR1 $29.95. Gun safety for the street, carry options, tactical draw, reloading, malfunction clearing for revolvers and semi-autos, magazine management, sighted and non-sighted accuracy, one-handed manipulation and firing, stopping power, basic combat shooting and firearm use, more.

Armed Response 4: Shoot/No Shoot Scenarios. #D-AR4 $29.95. 48 staged scenarios (like simulators use!) force you to react—should you draw, can you safely and legally fire? You really "get it" for bringing a gun into play in an armed confrontation. Each scene a life-like situation you could be in at home, work, shopping and more. Careful analysis follows every scene.

Armed Response 5: Responsible Use of Lethal Force. #D-AR5 $29.95. When to challenge, when to shoot, when not to shoot, legal principles examined. Escalation, reengagement and pursuit, disparity of force, Castle Doctrine, defense of third person, consequences of using force, finding an attorney, handling the aftermath.

WOMEN AND GUNS

From Luby's to the Legislature: One Woman's Fight Against Gun Control, Suzanna Gratia Hupp, 200 p., #FLT $22.95. The Luby's massacre in Texas could have been stopped by this woman, who had a clear shot at the murderer, but she left her gun in her car as required by law. Obeying that foolish law cost 23 lives, including her parents. She became a legislator and fought for gun laws that protect us instead of harm us. From naïve young woman to savvy freedom fighter, her amazing story in her own words, a superb read.

The Cornered Cat: A Woman's Guide to Concealed Carry. Kathy Jackson, 382 p., #CC, $19.95. Women don't fight like men. No bragging, threats or machismo, it's about getting away from danger as quickly as possible. The mindset is not me, not mine, not today, and whatever it takes to get out of harm's way. Packed with particulars on guns, carry, tactics, from a female perspective, by a trainer and editor of *Concealed Carry Magazine*, a truly excellent addition to the very limited literature for women and self defense.

Armed and Female. Paxton Quigley, 224 p., #AF, $19.95. She became an global celebrity when she first wrote *Armed and Female* in 1989. The first book of its kind—victim avoidance through armed resistance—by a woman, for women. Available again after years out of print, fully revised, better than ever. "I have trained 7,000 women aged 11 to 80 to shoot. Many were like me: scared or opposed to guns—and not wanting to think about using one. But they had a wake-up call... Mine was at 2 a.m. when I learned a close friend had been raped in her own home. I decided this would not happen to me..."

SELF DEFENSE

The Self-Defense Package. Various Authors, #SDP. $65.80 for all six books, save $20 when you buy this set! Come up to speed quickly with these all-around best-in-class books on the tactics and strategies of personal self defense and surviving an armed encounter. Prepare properly, anticipate trouble, avoid the fight if possible, win if it comes, deal with the aftermath. In The Gravest Extreme / Armed Response / How To Win A Gunfight / You and The Police / Principles of Personal Defense / Bonus: The Truth About Self Protection. Individual descriptions on our website, I assembled this set because it is the best.

After You Shoot: Your gun's hot, the perp's not, now what? Alan Korwin, 160 p., #AYS, $14.95. Dial 911 and fry... *Don't help convict yourself after self defense.* Legal loopholes and the justice system are poised to nail you, you can wind up in more trouble than the crook. Will you demand a lawyer—from the police who show up looking for convictions? Do you know what to say—since everyone says something? How do police squeeze guilty statements out of you? Jails are full of people who said the wrong things on 911 recordings. Includes aftermath procedures police themselves use. As important as the gun that saves your life.

In The Gravest Extreme. Massad Ayoob, 132 p. #ITGE $12.95. Widely recognized as the definitive work on the use of deadly force. This former law enforcement officer describes what you actually face in a lethal confrontation, a criminal's mindset, gun-fight tactics, judicial system's view on self-defense cases, more. Dispels the myths, truly excellent—a must for any armed household and especially CCW permitees.

The Concealed Handgun Manual. Chris Bird, 548 p. #CHM $24.95. A standard among concealed-handgun-permit holders—covers all the day-to-day details of licensed carry. The author intelligently discusses firearm choices, holster, carry method, dealing with the routine of staying armed. Good material on strategy, how to spot trouble coming and avoid it, what to expect afterwards, analysis of many actual self-defense shootings, and to top it off, a full 50-state guide to carry laws. A very worthwhile investment.

I'll bet you know someone who would benefit from the Q&A in this book.
Try this: lend your copy to that person when you're done.

The Truth About Self-Protection. Massad Ayoob, 418 p. #TASP $7.99. Get the facts on every aspect of personal safety, from evasive driving to planting cactus by your windows. Lifesaving techniques will help keep you, your family and your possessions safe, prepare you for defense if it becomes absolutely necessary, and guide you in buying lethal and less-than-lethal goods, from locks to firearms. Crime-avoidance techniques.

Armed Response. David Kenik. 178 p. #AR $19.95. A thorough guide for using firearms in self-defense. Practical, tactical info. Not standard training on safe and competent gun handling, here are plans, strategies and moves to win a gunfight—which never starts when you expect or goes the way you imagine. If you've got a solid stance and good sight picture, you're not moving fast enough or using cover properly.

No Second Place Winner. by Bill Jordan, hardcover, 114 p. #NSPW $14.95. An absolutely unique discussion of armed response by a man who literally made it his trade. Author Jordan worked the U.S. Border Patrol of the old days, for 30 years, and lived to tell about it. In the process, he became one of the deadliest shots of modern times. In an easy and unassuming way he describes with chilling clarity what it takes to come out on top of gun battles. "Be first or be dead... there are no second place winners." Packed with his personal tips on draw-and-shoot techniques, with wonderful stop-action photos.

GUN SAFETY AND POLITICS

Gun-Proof Your Children. Masaad Ayoob, 52 p. #GPYC $4.95. One of the world's leading experts on lethal-force issues, this father of two shares his thoughts and very practical ideas on gun safety for kids in a classic short booklet. Also includes a primer on hand- guns for the novice. Here is a parent's guide that does not advocate avoidance, and instead proposes that knowledge should trump ignorance, and that education is the best choice.

Thank God I Had A Gun. Chris Bird. 310 p. #TGI $19.95. The nationally acclaimed author of *The Concealed Handgun Manual* has put together 14 bone-chilling tales of people alive today because they had a firearm, loaded and ready, when the moment of truth arrived. Their bravery and successful tactics are lessons for the rest of us, helps dispel the "news" media nonsense that guns have no proper place in society.

The Bias Against Guns: Why Almost Everything You've Heard About Gun Control Is Wrong John R. Lott, Jr., Ph.D. Hardcover, #BAG $19.95. Dr. Lott has assembled hard proof for what so many of us have recognized—news media portrayal of guns and gun issues is completely wrong. They virtually exclude anything positive about guns, distort the rest. Millions of defensive gun uses (DGUs) occur annually, but the news in 2001 showed: USA Today: 5,660 words on gun crime, zero on DGUs; NY Times 50,745 words on gun crimes, DGUs 161 words (one story of an off-duty cop); All three networks combined, 190,000 to zero. Breathtaking facts.

More Guns, Less Crime. John R. Lott, Jr., Ph.D. 472 p. #MGLC $18.00. The classic. Lott, a scholar at Yale, became famous for it—a statistically sound, scientifically valid analysis of every American county, which found gun ownership lowers crime. He published the data, and other scholars confirmed the results. Anti-gun bigots hate this book because it shows gun ownership, specifically the right to carry, helps reduce crime. Packed with statistics, charts and graphs, but very readable and makes the point with crystal clarity—guns stop crime and deter criminals. New 3rd Edition.

Armed: New Perspectives on Gun Control. Gary Kleck, Don Kates, 360 p. #ANP $30.98. Hardcover. Studies show 700K to 2.5 million defensive gun uses every year (a fact the media hides). This book covers the 13 scholarly studies in plain English, with charts, analysis, legal and criminological evidence that refutes faulty assumptions driving gun-ban efforts. Great info on how guns are actually used and myths that circulate as fact.

GUN LAW

State by State Gun-Law Guides: Gun-law guides are independently produced by entrepreneurs in many states and we carry as many as we can find, in addition to books we publish. Order your state by mail, phone, or online at GunLaws.com. If your state is not available, consider one of the 50-state guides below.

#AZ $14.95; #CA $24.95; #FL $31.50; #IN $26.95; #KS $24.95; #MA $19.75; #MI $19.95; #MN $24.95; #MO1 $23.95; #MO2 $24.95; #MT $12.95; #NV $17.90; #NH $24.95; #NM $10.95; #NJ $49.95; #NY $36.95; #NC $25.00; #OH1 $19.95; #OH2 $19.95; #OR $12.95; #SC $19.95; #TN $14.95; #TX $14.95; #UT $18.71; #VA $14.95 #VT $15.00; #WA $10.95.

Traveler's Guide to Firearm Laws of the 50 States. Attorney J. Scott Kappas, 68 p. #TG $13.95. Because you are subject to arrest for simply traveling from state to state with a personal firearm, this guide is badly needed. This excellent book covers all the basics for armed travel: vehicles, glove box, open carry, permits, loaded or not, weapon types, state parks, restaurants, more. An indispensable tool if you travel armed and need the basics at each state line. Ranks each state on relative freedom too. Before you go, get and read this book. Includes the Nationwide Concealed Carry Reciprocity List!

Traveler's Gun and Knife Law Book. David Wong, 320 p., #TGAK, $14.95. If you travel armed, this is your book. If there is no gun guide for your state, this book is for you. If you want to see where the best laws are, this is your book. Like the classic *Traveler's Guide* people have used for years, but five times as thick to give you so much more detail—how to handle roadside stops, restaurant carry, carry on foot in parks, knife carry—all in plain English.

Self Defense Laws Of All 50 States. Mitch & Evan Vilos, 576 p., #SDL, $29.95. A stunning two-year achievement, never before attempted—the word-for-word laws plus plain-English coverage for self defense in every state—where you live and where you visit. Each state has its own chapter, state-to-state charts, with great detail on when deadly force is legally justifiable, and when shooting will get you busted. Case histories make the principles crystal clear. If you think you might ever need a gun to save your life, know the rules you face.

You & The Police. Boston T. Party, 168 p. #YATP $16. What should you do if stopped by police? Do you have to say if you're armed? Should you consent to a search? Can you talk your way out of a ticket? What are the rules on foot, or at home? This book answers these questions and more. Well researched, quotes actual cases, lets you emerge on top safely and with dignity.

BLOOMFIELD PRESS

4848 E. Cactus #505-440 • Scottsdale, AZ 85254
1-800-707-4020 Orders • 602-996-4020
info@gunlaws.com

GunLaws.com

Published by
BLOOMFIELD PRESS